CONCHIE

"*This is a searingly honest account of a son's efforts to comprehend his father's decision to be a conscientious objector rather than fight in the Second World War. He offers reasons not excuses, gives insights not alibis, details his own youthful embarrassment rather than pride, and shows deep respect for the courage of resolute conviction rather than exhibiting unconditional love. Because of that candour, readers will be left with greater understanding of "a different kind of courage" – and they might join me in having strengthened confidence in a rational system which wages war to defeat evil and, in doing that, protects the right of individuals to believe that it is wrong to fight and kill. The test of civilisation is, after all, not in the treatment of consenting majorities but in the toleration shown to non-conforming minorities.*"

– LORD NEIL KINNOCK

"*A fascinating insight into 1930s Welsh chapel culture, which formed the background to John Russell-Jones' decision to register as a conscientious objector in the Second World War.*"

– MARTYN WHITTOCK

Previous books by the author

My Secret Life in Hut Six
Sweet Tales from the Bitter Edge
Skeletons in Messiah's Cupboard
The Power of Ten

CONCHIE

What my father didn't do in the war

GETHIN RUSSELL-JONES

LION

Published by Lion Books
an imprint of
Lion Hudson plc
Wilkinson House, Jordan Hill Road,
Oxford OX2 8DR, England
www.lionhudson.com/lion

ISBN 978 0 7459 6854 4
e-ISBN 978 0 7459 6855 1

First edition 2016

Acknowledgments
Extracts from The Authorized (King James) Version. Rights in the Authorized
Version are vested in the Crown. Reproduced by permission of the Crown's
patentee, Cambridge University Press.
Scripture quotations marked NIV taken from the Holy Bible, New International
Version Anglicised. Copyright © 1979, 1984, 2011 Biblica, formerly
International Bible Society. Used by permission of Hodder & Stoughton Ltd, an
Hachette UK company. All rights reserved. "NIV" is a registered trademark of
Biblica. UK trademark number 1448790.

A catalogue record for this book is available from the British Library

Printed and bound in the UK, February 2016, LH26

Contents

Mummy and Daddy – you fought the good fight, finished the race and and kept the faith. May you rest in peace and rise in glory.

Family Tree

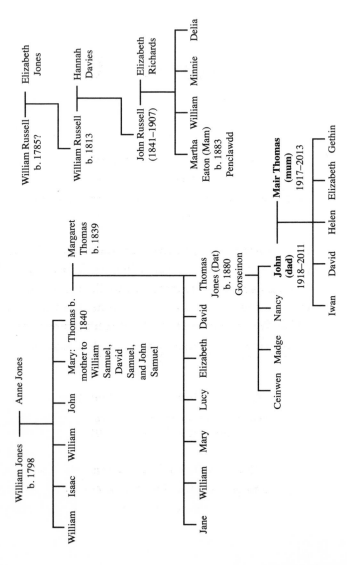

CHAPTER 1

War Child

**To kill Germans is a divine service
in the fullest sense of the word.**

*Archdeacon Basil Wilberforce, Chaplain to the Speaker of the
House of Commons (1914)*

**We are on the side of Christianity against anti-Christ.
We are on the side of the New Testament which respects
the weak, and honours treaties, and dies for its friends
and looks upon war as a regrettable necessity… It is a
Holy War, and to fight in a Holy War is an honour.**

*Right Reverend A. F. Winnington-Ingram, Bishop of London
(1914)*

Christ would have spat in your face.

*Anglican chaplain's words to an imprisoned conscientious objector
during World War One (1917)*

**But I say to you, love your enemies
and pray for those who persecute you.**

Jesus of Nazareth

This is what conscience looks like. It's a fourteen-year-old boy sitting anxiously on a sofa late in the afternoon. He's fondling a bloodstained tissue as his parents look at the purple swelling around his right eye. A knock on the front door and in comes his grammar school form teacher and out comes the story. My brother Iwan had been playing football that lunchtime, during which he had been assaulted by the school bully, who for no explicable reason punched him several times in the face. To the consternation of everyone, Iwan had not retaliated and had walked away with a bloodied nose and mouth. None of his friends understood his reaction and neither apparently had his teacher. So this was his question to my brother: "Iwan, why didn't you fight back? You were entitled to defend yourself. This question has been bothering me since school ended and I had to ask you." Iwan, who has never been a timid soul, had a clear and surprising answer. "It was the way I was brought up, sir, never to take revenge on anyone. It would have gone against my conscience."

This book is about the power of conscience and the way it influenced my family's story. In particular it's about my father's life before, during, and after World War Two. I'm going to tell the stories of the people, events, and ideas that shaped a decision he took as a 21-year-old man; a decision that still reaches into his family years after his death.

Most of us over the age of fifty have a war story. In one way or another, our fathers and some of our mothers were involved in the Second World War, willingly or not. And whether alive or dead our grandfathers also gave report of life and death in the First World War, the Great War. Beneath the largely peaceable skies of the northern hemisphere, we are only one generation removed from events that rocked the world and shaped the culture we inhabit.

Take my friend Dave for example. As we sit sipping coffee and he munches on a teacake, he asks me about this book. I explain it's about pacifism during World War Two. He then discloses two extraordinary war tales. His father, Ron Clague, was one of the first to liberate Dachau, whose infamy as a Nazi death camp has gone down in history. Such was the disfiguring and deadly evil witnessed by this twenty-year-old, that he barely spoke about it. Dave talked also about Ron's best friend, Ernie. As a teenager, Dave casually asked Ernie what he had done in the war and he received a reply that had never been given until that moment. Holding back tears and trying to contain big, painful emotions, Ernie talked about the Death Railway, made famous in the films *The Bridge on the River Kwai* and *The Railway Man*. Captured as a prisoner of war by the Japanese, he was forced to work on the vast railway that stretched from Ban Pong in Thailand to Thanbyuzayat in Myanmar (Burma). It was a brutal and torturous regime and many POWs were beaten to death. There were also a huge number of deaths among the Romusha, Asian civilians forced to work on the railroad. Over 12,000 British, Allied, and American servicemen alone lost their lives. It is said that for every piece of track laid, someone died.

A few days later and I am having coffee with Martin, another friend. In the course of our conversation, I casually mention the subject of this book and he drops a bombshell. His grandfather Maurice Allen was a conscientious objector (CO) in the First World War, whilst his father Dennis was a CO in the Second.

I too have a story; I'm just not sure whether I like it that much.

CHAPTER 2

Conchie

My dad, John Russell-Jones, was a CO (or Conchie as they were usually called) in World War Two. I want to open the sealed envelope of my father's account, get behind the story, and find the 21-year-old young man who was prepared to face such opposition. This quest is given added bite by the looming centenary of an Act of Parliament that made my father's dissent, and that of many thousands like him, possible.

As World War One went on, and newspapers reported the thousands of casualties suffered by the armed forces, and mutilated soldiers returned home, Britain increasingly lost its appetite for glory on the field of battle. Widely circulating accounts of chlorine, phosgene, and mustard gassing in the trenches added to the public's distaste for military service. Whereas nearly 1.5 million men had volunteered during the first six months of the war, numbers had dropped dramatically by 1915, and continued to do so.

It was the day that saw the death of the happy amateur, the gentleman volunteer. After two years of warfare with Germany, the numbers of men enlisting to fight for king and empire were dwindling. No longer able to resist conscription, Prime Minister Asquith relented and on 2 March 1916 the Military Service Act came into force, having been passed in January. Much to the chagrin of the Liberal Party, Labour Party, and Trades Union Congress, the new law represented the failure of several voluntary schemes. Military service was now compulsory for all men between the ages of eighteen and forty-one, although there were a number of exempt categories: married men, widowers with children, men in reserved occupations, and clergy.

And a new exemption was created: that of the conscientious objector. Virtually alone on the world stage, Britain allowed men to appeal against conscription on the grounds of conscience. A handful of nations gave exemptions to Mennonites and Quakers but none recognized the right to dissent on broader religious and moral grounds. So this was a groundbreaking moment in British legal history on two counts; conscription was introduced for the first time, as was the right to resist it.

But still the numbers enlisting were not sufficient for the war effort, so the Act was revised four months later. All men previously declared medically unfit for service were to be re-examined, and retired servicemen were also included within its provisions. In 1917 the Act was again changed: servicemen who had left military service due to ill health were to be re-examined, as were Home Service Territorials, and the list of reserved occupations was shortened.

But still they wouldn't come and so the legal stick was further strengthened in January 1918 with further amendments. Various occupational and other exemptions were quashed, and yet the war needed far greater numbers. So in April 1918, with the war now reaching its apex and the burial grounds of the Western Front filling with the fallen dead, the parameters were dramatically changed. Men aged between seventeen and fifty-one were now conscripted and for the first time this extended to Ireland (although the policy was never implemented there), the Channel Islands, and the Isle of Man.

Three million men volunteered for military service between August 1914 and when the first version of the Military Service Act came into force in 1916. A further 2.3 million men were conscripted as a result of legal coercion.

Globally, over 17 million men died in the Great War and a further 37 million were wounded. At least 887,711 United Kingdom and Colonies military personnel were killed and when civilian deaths were added, the UK casualty figure rose to over a million.

Conscription was abolished in 1919 but reintroduced in May 1939 before the outbreak of war with Germany. The Military Training Act required all men aged twenty and twenty-one to be called up for military duty, although this was superseded in September when the National Service (Armed Forces) Act came into force. All men aged between eighteen and forty were required to sign up for duty and, after extensive loss of life, this age limit was extended to fifty-one at the end of 1941. From 1941 onwards and for the first time in the history of the British Isles, single women aged twenty to thirty were also compelled to perform non-combatant duties.

All these legislative measures recognized the rights of conscientious objectors (COs) and prescribed the means by which their appeals could be heard and judged. In the First World War there were 16,000 registered Conchies and there were 61,000 in World War Two. And it is not unfair to say that as a group they were generally reviled and misunderstood. Many of the COs in both wars objected on the basis of religious conviction, but others said no for political and moral reasons.

I'm going to try and find out why my father followed the voice of conscience instead of the prime minister's.

My dad was not a killer; that much I do know. However, even though his war passed without salute, parade, or medal he served in a different way: protecting others without lifting a rifle. Not so my mother. Her world war came to an end sometime in the 1990s; in that decade she broke her long silence and began to break the hold of the Official Secrets Act. Initially a trickle and finally as a broken cataract, she spoke of Bletchley Park and her part in Hitler's downfall.

Whereas my mother kept mum for over a generation and then spoke of nothing but the war for the last ten years of her life, my father was different. His running commentary started as Germany invaded Poland, gathered pace during his student years, and then petered out in his later adult life.

Within the confines of home, he could sometimes be volubly critical of war, always advocating a more Christian perspective as he saw it. His pacifism was bundled together with republicanism, socialism, and a general dislike of any kind of privilege. In public, however, he was a model of diplomacy; except on one very public occasion when he cocked a snook at the establishment.

I need to find out why my father refused to fight in the Second World War, especially as this decision heaped criticism on him and his parents. Not unlike him, I've largely kept quiet about his Conchie status outside the home. So this quest will also probe my own reactions. Why have I kept so silent? Am I embarrassed, ashamed even? From a young age I knew that Dad was a pacifist; it's my reaction that's the problem. But there's another aspect to all this: whereas I can recall his pacifist leanings, not all my siblings can. This is why tracing any family's narrative is more or less doomed to be a two-headed fact and myth creation. So what follows is my take on my dad's dissent; I cannot claim it as the authorized version.

The publication of my book about my mother's wartime heroism, *My Secret Life in Hut Six*, and the seventy-fifth anniversary of the D-Day landings in 2014 have forced me to look again at my father's legacy of non-violence. On the day of the seventy-fifth anniversary, the TV schedules were filled with men of his generation: grey, distinguished, and lauded for their courage. There was even the story of 89-year-old Bernard Jordan, a World War Two veteran who escaped from his care home on the south coast of England and travelled to Normandy to be part of the celebrations. Without a formal invite and without the home's permission, he took a ferry to France and became an overnight national treasure.

All the men were of my father's vintage, each with a story to tell. Whiskery, grey, and beret-capped, they looked back to a time when they took on the world. Like him, many of them became fathers and grandfathers and had known long professional lives. But they had faced a terrifying rain of bullets, bombs, grenades, and landmines and somehow survived. They came also to remember fallen comrades whose bodies now lie in foreign soil. Not so with my father. No stories of adventure, fear, or tedium; his world war was a very personal affair.

His legacy of pacifism sits uneasily with me and I'd like to know why he chose not to bear arms against the Germans and their allies. During my teenage years when teachers and other boys spoke openly of wartime connections, I kept my counsel. In more recent times my disquiet over the pacifism of my now dead father has grown. So this book is an investigation on two levels. I'm searching for clues about my father's decision to stand up and not be counted as a soldier. I also want to understand and deal with my own warring feelings.

There have been times when I have admired his lonely, even heroic bravery. Not going along with popular opinion and having a dissenting voice is a deeply uncomfortable thing to do, especially when your actions are perceived as unpatriotic and weak. That takes a certain kind of courage. Particularly when I consider that my father was socially compliant, reserved, and conservative (with a small "c").

I remember him as an old man: suited, aged, and blind. Quiet, dignified, he bore his sightlessness with great stoicism. Firm, often dogmatic, he was yet willing to find common ground with others. I want to reach back to his earlier outspoken bachelor years, and get beyond the guarded man, often suspicious of others, anxious about losing his reputation and messing it all up. I need to travel back to another age where he swam against the prevailing tide. I'm looking for a stubborn hothead; at least that's the image in my mind. I need to peel back the layers, see beyond the various versions and copies that I and others have made. This is of course well-nigh impossible; in the end, our reputation is the sum total of what others think of us.

My cousin Gareth Morris published a small book during his seventieth year, a volume of poetry and prose catching each day of those twelve months. In it he reminisces about the mythical image of my father, known to him as Wncwl (Uncle) John. Gareth's mother Madge was my dad's oldest sister, and she died in 1992. Speaking of that generation, he says:

> They always wanted to be seen to be doing the right thing
> and the chief arbiter of what was acceptable seemed to be
> Uncle John whether he was present or not. My mother
> would say to me as a child, if I spoke to her cheekily,
> "Uncle John would never have spoken to Mam like that!"
> Or if I was slightly unwilling to run a message, "Uncle
> John used to clean the grate and lay the fire before going

to school." I had such a strong impression that Uncle John was perfection personified that when, as a rather naive nine-year-old, an older boy introduced me graphically to the facts of life, I thought to myself "Uncle John would never do a thing like that," even though I was fully aware that he was already the father of three children.[1]

And it's that perception of him that I've come across all my life, giving an added zest to my inquiry.

My brother Iwan has a further comment to add to Gareth's observation:

He knew he was regarded as a paragon of virtue by his family and he couldn't stomach it! I think he felt that he was as flawed as everyone else and certainly no better than anyone.

My dad never seemed to be, nor behaved like, a political activist and maybe he wasn't. It could be that his sense of right conduct on all occasions rose out of his strong conviction about Christian morality and this included the duty not to fight. He also felt strongly about the duty not to consume alcohol, smoke tobacco, have sex outside marriage, and the need to vote for the Labour Party at all times.

As an adolescent I felt the strangeness of his pacifist viewpoint. As the youngest of five children, most of my friends had much younger fathers. Born in 1918, John was fifty by the time I was eight years old. My friends' fathers belonged to a different generation; they listened to popular music and wore younger clothes. To the day of his death, my dad was most comfortable in a jacket and tie and his experience of modern music extended to Benjamin Britten, although we did also possess a copy of Herb Albert's Tijuana jazz hymns. Military life for other dads had largely come through National Service, although there were a few friends whose fathers had fought in the war. I wondered why mine hadn't. They had military photographs on their pianos: men in smiling khaki looking ahead to a brighter future. All we had were his powerful and oft-rehearsed arguments reflecting his Christian and political bias. Photographs of him from that period invariably picture him young and suited. But still I wonder how he could have been prepared to let Hitler in by the front door.

I recall an incomprehensible Physics lesson in 1974. The teacher assigned some sort of task involving ticker tape which I failed to complete in the company of a fellow pupil, Mark. Instead we talked about my parents. I'd spoken to him before and counted him a friend, but his tone that morning was hostile, biting. He poured scorn on my father's profession as a minister, preferring his dad's occupation as a fireman. This he said was a useful trade, helping many, whereas my dad probably did nothing from one Sunday to another. He wouldn't listen to my counter-arguments. Somehow the conversation moved to the war. It transpired that his dad had fought in World War Two, North Africa he thought. What had mine done? I reddened, felt awkward as my collar moistened. I replied that he had been a conscientious objector. Never heard of it, what's one of those? A pacifist – refused to fight on moral grounds because he was a Christian. Ridicule and laughter followed. What sort of man was my father? Did he agree with Hitler? Didn't he care? At least he believed in something unlike your fireman dad who went along with the crowd. It takes courage to be different and unpopular; I bet your dad hasn't thought about anything important in his life. This exchange inevitably ended in a fight.

However, it's Mark's voice that has plagued me when it comes to this matter. Setting aside the nasty tone that still resonates thirty-five years later, I can't help siding with the sentiment of his accusations. Compared to the tearful farewell and triumphant return of the gallant soldiers, my dad just stayed, said no, and got on with his life. It's hard to find anything heroic or noble in this choice.

In my darker moods, I conclude that my father saved himself but let others perish. In salving his own conscience, he showed little concern for the hundreds of thousands locked in mortal combat. Utterly convinced that it was absolutely wrong at all times to kill another human being, he read of the death of others and did nothing to intervene. Thus my admiration of him is tempered by feelings of embarrassment and even shame. In his later life he could be an ardent champion of social justice and defender of religious freedom. But at this crucial period in his life, he prized his own individual rights over and above the needs of the community. That's how it seems to me. Knowing that my father did nothing to engage with the global menace of Nazism is deeply uncomfortable to me.

This is how he once explained his position to me:

I didn't like Nazism any more than anyone else, or the thought of living under Hitler's rule. But my conscience forbade me from taking another human life, whatever the reason. I would have killed other human beings whose lives were as sacred as mine. I would have fought other Christians, like me; making enemies of people who were my brothers! It would have been difficult but I didn't see any military solution to the problem.

His pledge was not to a flag or nation but to another king. He believed that following Jesus Christ meant a life of challenge and dissent: of forgiveness, non-violence, and reconciliation. And no politician or war could overturn his understanding of what it meant to be a Christian. Being a conscientious objector was not about cowardice but a logical outcome of faith.

So I'm on the hunt for the truth. What led him to choose Christ above Churchill? What does this period in his life tell me about him? Did cowardice or appeasement play a part in his decision? It seems to me that most sons, maybe all children, struggle with their parents in life and death. This is my attempt to make sense of my dad.

But there are less silent witnesses. Family members who remember him as a young man will speak of dissent, radical politics, passionate religion, and a man incapable of taking a life. Another relative is adamant about this: "Everyone knew Uncle John couldn't go to war. He just wasn't that sort of man, the killing kind."

But another relative, a historian, takes exception to this. She says:

I don't think anyone is naturally a soldier, or able to kill more easily than others. Most of the men I've read about who went to war were terrified at the prospect but went along with it whether through a sense of duty or peer pressure.

And this is my greatest fear: that I will discover that my father's real motivation was cowardice. That beyond his philosophy of non-violence and ethical Christianity, I will find a man terrified at having to leave college cloisters and chapel vestries for military duty. That the man I find will be all too human.

My siblings have their own recollections of his pacifism and there are others who will speak of the culture of radical Christian dissent that cradled him and has all but disappeared. Ultimately in this crowded gallery of people and stuff, I'm hoping to find the biggest answer. Why did he do it? Actually, the question I really want to address is even more fundamental: who was my father?

The late brilliant lawyer and writer John Mortimer wrote a biography of his dad called *A Voyage Around My Father*. And this is my journey into my father's mind. My father was a religious man and he understood himself and the world through the lens of his belief. But don't let that put you off, particularly if you are not of his religion or any other. It's about a son trying to understand his dad: a very basic human quest whatever your view of God.

I'm going to tell his story largely through the silent witnesses that have survived him: diaries, press cuttings, photographs, remembered conversations, his books, and the stories of family members. I'm going to connect the various fragments of the story by asking questions of the bric-a-brac that surrounded him: parts I'm familiar with and the perplexing gaps. It's at this point I wish I had the treasure trove of material afforded to Edmund de Waal in *The Hare with Amber Eyes*. Readers of that book will remember that the author traces his illustrious family's history by means of a set of netsukes bequeathed to him by his uncle. Netsukes are Japanese porcelain miniatures, traditionally used by monks to tie around their belts. Carved in the shape of sundry animals and humans, they had been in his family for centuries. This award-winning book follows the journey of this collection as the family travels around the great cities of Europe, as well as the Orient. It's a breathtaking adventure, taking us into grand palaces in Vienna and Paris, following the fortunes and losses of this wealthy Jewish banking family across the continent. The netsukes are mute witnesses to fabulous wealth and ultimately to the despair of Nazi-occupied Austria with its brutal anti-Semitism.

Not so with me. There is no one single collection that will help me now. In many ways, my search has more in common with BBC Radio Four's *History of the World in a Hundred Objects* or *Germany: Memories of a Nation*. Both of these programmes were presented by Neil MacGregor, former director of the British Museum. And the device used was simple. What do these objects tell us about the era in which they were invented and the people who used them, and how do they influence us today? That will be my approach.

There are family objects and photographs from that period. A few recordings of my father survive: interviews with one of his grandsons and a small number of monologues recorded after he went totally blind in 2000. My father's nieces and nephews (a generation older than me who remember him as a young man during the war) have their own fascinating accounts of his behaviour in that period. And there are anecdotes and family tales, plenty of them, handed down and in circulation among my siblings and me. Many of the fragments are his recollections, rehearsed regularly in my hearing and told in his voice, as recalled by me and others.

My dad's part in Hitler's downfall is complicated. His war was very different from that of the three and a half million men who fought in the armed forces. During one vivid period of his life, he swam against the raging torrent of public opinion and followed his own convictions. He was barely twenty-one, had never left Wales, and was not yet a student. At the same age some of his contemporaries were bearing arms, sailing ships, and piloting aeroplanes in a desperate bid to protect Britain from invasion.

I will narrate the story, but there are many places where the print is in italic. This is my father's voice: words transcribed from his writings or recordings, or as recalled by me and others who knew him. Other voices and quotations will not be italicized.

To completely misquote an Old Testament prophet commanded by the Almighty to enliven a valley of dry bones, I too want these dead papers and objects to live and tell the strange story of war.

By the time he died, my father had celebrated sixty-five years as an ordained church minister within the Baptist denomination. Alongside my mother, this was his greatest passion, yet sometimes the ministry was his worst pain. He was an enigma; often disengaged in home life, occasionally the beating heart of it all; distracted by other matters, frequently unwell, obsessed with his work, acutely aware of his public reputation even in his most private moments; and the best raconteur bar none. To thousands of others, he was a gifted preacher, whose oratory and learning inspired many. I want to get beyond all this noise, in search of that belligerent, vulnerable, peaceable, and angry 21-year-old who said no to his country in its hour of need. A man full of contradictions, who loved the church and yet felt like an outsider for all his life.

Was he outspoken or simply an outsider?

CHAPTER 3

A Good Year for Diaries

It was the year my legal career finally miscarried and my father nearly died of exhaustion. In 1983 I failed my Bar exams and realized I would never be the Rumpole of the Bailey of my generation. In that year my father also retired as a Baptist minister. After decades of forceful preaching, sucking up the bitter poisons of religious disputes and wading through the detritus of human misery, he was forced to stop working before it killed him.

Medical opinion persuaded him that unless he retired immediately he would probably suffer major respiratory and cardiac problems, and die. A lifetime in the damp and smog of the South Wales valleys had taken its toll. Mix that with a heady cocktail of overwork, endless conflict management, and perfectionist tendencies, and this was the way it was bound to end.

In August of that year my parents moved to a new house provided by their denomination for the use of retired ministers and their families. It was a pretty little detached house, but woefully small for the library of books and papers my dad had amassed over the years. A decision was taken – a temporary one and only for a week or two until all this material could be housed somewhere else. His collection would all be kept in my sister's garage down the road: a draughty concrete-built construction complete with a drop-down steel door. Some makeshift shelves were constructed, and the rest stuffed into suitcases, a trunk, and even a wardrobe. All very provisional we said; his pride and joy would soon be dispersed in all our various houses and out of the elements. His children were however inconsistent and it all stayed in the garage. All except for the diary he was keeping that year.

Unusually, my dad kept a daily diary in 1983. Most of his others were a mixture of blank pages, endless sermon notes, jottings, and random accounts of events and feelings. But in that year he chose to narrate each day's events and reflections. And it was a good year for diaries. On 23 April, *The Sunday Times* and German magazine *Stern* went public with their intentions to publish the newly discovered Hitler Diaries. It was the publishing scoop of the century. *Stern* purchased the diaries and sold serialization rights to *The Sunday Times*, *Newsweek*, *Paris Match*, and a range of other European print media. Rupert Murdoch, owner of *The Sunday Times*, paid over a million dollars for the rights. Murdoch's confidence in the veracity of the diaries came from the endorsement given by Lord Dacre (Hugh Trevor-Roper), one of *The Sunday Times'* independent directors. However, at the press conference on 23 April when this news was made public, Lord Dacre announced that he had grave doubts about the provenance of the diaries. Despite this, Murdoch authorized the publication of the first extracts on 25 April. The controversy, however, unravelled and it turned out that the whole project was fraudulent. The diaries were the work of a German forger, Konrad Kujau, who managed to get his forgeries into the hands of a *Stern* journalist, Geid Heidemann, who had persuaded his employers to buy the diaries.

Unlike Kujau's deception, the diaries now in my possession bear the authentic traits of my father's voice. In his words I hear him once again; notes, scribblings, doodles, and sermon ideas, found in exercise books, diaries, scraps of paper, and on the back of agendas and minutes. There are musty, fading press cuttings, some from the First World War. Thankfully my parents were hoarders and their stories can be traced through inky jottings and newsprint. Gathering mildew and damp, the collection remained in my sister's garage until 2011 when my father died at the age of ninety-two.

So my journey begins with his 1983 diary. Compared to much of the other material, this volume is in good condition. Unlike the rest, it remained on my dad's dry shelves, unexposed to the damp misery of the garage. It's a proper diary: red, hardback, page a day. On the inside is an inscription: "To Mr Jones, with best wishes from the sisters of the Sisterhood, Mount Carmel."

He was the minister of Mount Carmel Baptist Church, Caerphilly, and this was a gift from the women's meeting. He kept it religiously for most of the year and it marked a seemingly new beginning in his journaling. A decade or more had passed since his last diary and as he approached his final year of work before claiming the old-age pension, he was trying to make sense of his life and faith. And I want you to meet my dad in his own words. There's plenty of religious material of course, but there are equal amounts of political satire and very tender vignettes of family life. And he could at times be wickedly funny. Here is his assessment of a sermon he had to endure at a civic event on Sunday 12 June:

*Horace Rowland is the chairman of the Rhymney Valley
Council for the coming year and there was a civic service
in Mount Carmel in the afternoon. There was quite a*

good congregation, but there was little in the sermon for
anyone. Based on the glorious 103 Psalm, the utterance was
irrelevant to the occasion, was devoid of any semblance of
theology and lacked even the barest reference to the Lord
Jesus Christ... I suppose it takes a genius of sorts to speak
on this psalm without even the most oblique reference
to the God to whom all praise belongs. There was no
"liberalism", or "radicalism", or "modernism". There was just
nothingarianism.

In this, his final salaried year, he referred several times to his deep sense of "calling". Apart from a brief period as a sales assistant in a gentlemen's outfitter as a teenager, and a year's college teaching in his fifties, he had been a Baptist minister for all of his working life. For him, there was no greater vocation than to preach Christ and serve his people. This for him was the most elevated occupation of all. For example, one of his favourite historical figures was William Carey, the first missionary to India and founder of the Baptist Missionary Society. Carey, a Northampton cobbler, took his wife and numerous children to India in the seventeenth century. He has gone down in church history as an apostle to the subcontinent, even though his wife went insane and his children had to fend for themselves. He had hoped that his son Felix would follow in his steps and become a missionary, but his political ambitions took priority, leading his father to say: "my son set out as a minister of Christ; but alas! He has dwindled down to a mere British ambassador."

My father loved that quotation.

As he approached retirement, he received a questionnaire from the South Wales Baptist College, surveying the views of ordained clergy throughout Wales. There were numerous questions about locality, stipend, length of service, and the type of ministry being exercised. But the last question was the most interesting: "Is the call to ordained ministry permanent or are there circumstances where the minister may leave this office for other employment?"

His reply was terse:

This is the highest calling and the greatest privilege. There are no circumstances which allow a minister to turn their back on this call.

This is how he looked back on his life as a church minister on 5 July 1983:

How good to be reminded of that initial call! Unbelievably it came to me. What was involved in it I understood very imperfectly and it was with the passing of the years that I came to realise that my calling was to servanthood – servant of Christ, servant of the Word, servant of the church. Those titles seem to me to sum up the essence of the Christian ministry in the prophetic, priestly and pastoral aspects... how humbling to be reminded that having done all, I have not "arrived". Far from attaining perfection either in life or ministry, like that far more devoted minister, Paul, I am just pressing on to take hold of that for which Christ Jesus took hold of me.

He ended with a short Latin phrase used by the famous Victorian preacher Charles Haddon Spurgeon as the motto for his preachers' college in London: *TENEO ET TENEOR,* I hold and I am held.

Tucked away in one of the pages of this diary is his first handwritten letter of resignation to the church he has served and now must leave. Here is part of that letter:

More than forty-six years have gone by since I heard the call to the ministry and for thirty-eight years it has been my privilege to be a servant of the Lord Jesus Christ and of his Word and of his church. It is my constant wonder that as Paul says, "to me, though I am the very least of the saints, this grace was given, to preach the unsearchable riches of Christ," and that in Trefforest, Aberystwyth, Risca, Llanelli, Cardiff and Caerphilly.

This year is a good place to start. There are intriguing references to the war and insights into his state of mind at that time. But as I read his entries, I am once again struck by the complexity of my dad. Funny, poignant, a family man who also comes across as a loner. A man of faith moved by his own and others' fragility. Here's another flavour, taken from his entry on Wednesday 9 February, at the age of sixty-four, worrying about the prospect of retirement:

There are times when I am plagued by the thought that I have been woefully remiss in not providing for our future. But bringing up five children on a shoe string budget has allowed no room for saving. However, the Lord has provided for our needs in the past and we safely trust the future to him.

My father was deep feeling and reflective, given to periods of guilt and sometimes depression. But rarely did he express any of these feelings to his family, except presumably to Mum. When I think of him, and that's every day, I remember someone comfortable in a professional persona but not in his own skin. But in his diaries, the guard was dropped and the real man shines through the pages. Rarely did he air his political views from the pulpit, but on Monday 16 May 1983, the first working day after Parliament was dissolved ahead of the general election, he commented on the Conservative Party's prospects:

> *... I wonder if they really believe what they say. How can they talk of solid achievements when they set their meagre achievements against the promises that carried them into power at the last election? We stand for law and order they said – and we've had Toxteth and Brixton and a growing crime rate. Bring down unemployment they said – and it's almost trebled. Cut the taxes they said – and they did for the highly paid wealthy minority but for the many caught in the poverty trap there was no relief. This has been a most divisive government and one could not envisage it being re-elected for a further term if the Labour Party had provided an effective opposition. So torn has that party been however by internecine feuds and conflicting policies, so weakened by the defection of some of its most effective spokesmen to the SDP, so unsure of its direction, that it cannot inspire much confidence.*

Sadly for my father, Margaret Thatcher's Tory Party won a landslide victory, taking 397 seats to Labour's 209. Labour's beleaguered leader, Michael Foot, blamed the SDP for siphoning away traditional socialist votes, and David Steel, the head of the Liberal Party, blamed the electoral system for their poor showing. Thus it ever was.

Dad was a passionate, fluent orator. Like all good public speakers, he built his argument through repeating short memorable statements, using increasing irony before delivering the killer blow. Dad the radical, always on the side of the squashed and overlooked. Dad the pundit, eager to share his wisdom about political matters.

And yet, beyond the home he was neutral, silent, and eager to keep the ship steady. This was his public front, the one he slipped into most of the time: measured, cautious, even suspicious.

This 1983 diary also recorded several military items of news on which he commented. His tone was sceptical, acid at times. In the first month of the year, the government's review of the 1982 Falklands War was published. Under the chairmanship of Lord Franks, the committee looked into the build-up to the Argentine invasion of the Falklands and subsequent British actions. Its conclusions were favourable towards the Conservative government, and my father was not impressed:

It was presented to the House of Commons by Mrs Thatcher. She was obviously cock a hoop at what appears to be an almost complete vindication of the Government in its handling of events leading up to the Falklands War. There will be many who will not be able to enter into her mood of exaltation and suspect that what they feared since the setting up of the Franks Commission six months ago has indeed taken place viz the whitewashing of the whole sorry business...

The themes, values, and beliefs that shaped him can be seen here; his socialist tendencies, deep opposition to war, and way with words. The theme of war surfaced again in February when he commented on a debate held in the Church of England synod on the church and the bomb. It was a period of heightened military awareness and protest in Britain particularly as the Falklands War had divided opinion. After the government's decision to allow American cruise missiles to be kept on British soil in 1981, a female-led protest took place at Greenham Common, by the missile base, and it was given daily news coverage. In April 1983,

70,000 women formed a human chain around the perimeter fence. My dad's interest in the synod debate displayed a balanced view of the issue:

I heard parts of the debate on the radio and was tremendously impressed both by the spirit in which it was conducted and the quality of the speeches. The result was a victory for the multilateralists, perhaps predictably, but on both sides there seemed to be a desire to be Christian and rational rather than jingoistic and emotional.

Christian, rational, not given to emotionalism: a fitting summary of my father's character. He could also be defensive, avoidant, and freeze you with silence. As a young man in 1939, he made a public choice that set him at odds with most of the Western world, and on Monday 31 January 1983 he made reference to the dominating tone of that period:

It came as a shock to be reminded that 50 years ago this past weekend, Adolf Hitler became Chancellor of Germany. I was then a lad of 14 and a half, probably in the fourth form at Gowerton County Intermediate School. I remember over the years the Reichstag fire, instigated by the Nazis and the farcical trial of the accused Communists. A 14 year old could hardly have imagined how the influence and power of Hitler and his henchmen would escalate in the next few years – and indeed very few of maturer years were alive to the menace. None the less, I remember the chill that struck my adolescent heart on seeing the photographs in the Daily Herald *of the Führer addressing the mass meetings of his jack booted, goose stepping, Heil Hitlering followers...*

CHAPTER 4

Strong Mothers

Painted by Sidney Curnow Vosper in 1908, *Salem* depicted Sunday worship at a Baptist chapel in North Wales. Along with *Taith y Pererin* (Welsh translation of *The Pilgrim's Progress*) and Bishop William Morgan's Welsh Bible, this painting was part of a trinity of cultural icons found in most homes in Wales in the early years of the twentieth century. And it made its way into our family.

Having already tasted international success as a watercolour artist, Vosper turned his attention to Welsh subjects after his marriage to Merthyr-born Constance James in 1902. Set three years after the end of the Welsh revival, the picture portrayed a number of pious souls preparing for worship. Only one of the figures was actually a member of the chapel: Robert Williams of Caer Meddyg, a carpenter, farmer, and deacon at Capel Salem, visible on the far left beneath the clock. Next to him and slightly obscured was Laura Williams of Ty'n-y-Buarth, Llanfair. Left of her, with his back against the wall, was Owen Jones (commonly called Owen Siôn) of Carreg Coch. The small boy was Evan Edward Lloyd and by his side was Mary Rowland. On the extreme right, with his head bowed, was William Jones (William

Siôn), brother of Owen. Vosper paid each model sixpence an hour for sitting.

The main figure was Siân Owen, who at the time of painting was seventy-one and lived in remote countryside near Lampeter. A widow, she raised two sons in her tiny cottage, although they were both later killed in the First World War. Siân Owen lived until 1927, and then was buried in a Harlech churchyard.

The eighth figure (second right of Siân Owen, wearing a traditional Welsh hat) was a borrowed tailor's dummy which Vosper named "Leusa Jones". The chapel elders were uncomfortable with the dummy being in a place of worship, insisting that it was to be removed each Saturday night before the "Seiat" (weekly church meeting) the following morning.

My grandparents, Tom and Mattie (Martha) Jones, owned a copy of *Salem*, which hung in their home in Brynhyfryd Road, Gorseinon. We referred to them as Mam and Dat, Dat being an abbreviated version of *Datgu*, Welsh for grandfather, and Mam being the shorter form of *Mamgu*. This painting was given to my parents as a wedding present in 1946 and thereafter adorned the lounges of the many manses we lived in as we grew up.

It's an eerie and strange painting and as a child I found it frightening. The figures are so severe and silent, powerfully disapproving of any incorrect behaviour. And it contains several enigmas. The clock on the wall shows that it has gone ten o'clock and the faithful few are already in silence before the imminent start of the meeting. Siân Owen is late and this, accompanied by her expensive shawl, suggests that she wants to be noticed. This may be Vosper's nod to religious hypocrisy. But there are supernatural references in this piece. From the very beginning, people have seen the devil's face in Siân Owen's shawl, even though Vosper denied deliberately placing it there. He did however acknowledge painting a ghostly face outside the window, a phantom witness to this quiet sabbath in Wales.

But the painting proved to be wildly popular in the UK and beyond. In large part this was due to the marketing genius of the painting's buyer, William Hesketh Lever. Lever bought *Salem* in 1909 and used the image to promote his star product, Lever Brothers' Sunlight Soap. This happy marriage of product and image led to one of Britain's first consumer loyalty schemes. Each bar of soap came with collectable tokens, and customers who bought seven pounds' worth of Sunlight Soap could exchange these for a print of *Salem*. This commercial genius resulted in the mass production of Vosper's religious work and ensured that working-class homes in Wales had their own work of art on display. This is how it came to be in the possession of my grandparents. An artist who had exhibited in the salons of Paris had inadvertently enabled the workers of Wales to start their own collections.

This depiction of a strong independent woman speaks to me of the greatest political influences on my father. Whenever I asked him who had inspired him in his pacifism, his reply was always the same: his paternal grandmother Margaret and his own mother Martha.

Margaret Thomas was illiterate and only spoke Welsh. She failed to read a single book to the day of her death and yet this woman from west Wales was part of a radical stream of thought that believed that it was humanity's duty to build God's kingdom on earth and turn swords into ploughshares.

Nothing about Margaret's life suggested she would become highly influential, at least to her grandson. Born in 1850, in the small hamlet of Ffald-y-Brenin in rural Carmarthenshire on the slopes of the Black Mountains, she lived and died within a pony and cart's journey of this hilly county. Even then the countryside was pouring its youth into the new urban hotspots of Swansea and Merthyr. As a young woman she was taken into the service of a noted county family by the name of Richard – wealthy landowners who were prominent nonconformists, and liberal in politics. Although this new middle class were few in number across Wales, the Richard family's values were mirrored throughout the nation. This was the culture that bred and nurtured David Lloyd George, the only Welshman to hold the highest political office in Great Britain. Following Asquith's resignation he would lead his country through the First World War and show little favour to the arguments put forward by conscientious objectors.

The Richard family farmed in the lush dairy land along the River Cothi. One of the fragments of Margaret's memories handed carefully down to successive generations is an eyewitness account of religious revival:

> She told me that one Sunday afternoon she was out walking;
> it was the only afternoon off she had in the week and she
> would go to chapel in the evening. She could hear the sound
> of singing and as she turned a bend in the river, she saw
> hundreds of people on the bank opposite and a man standing
> in the water. He must have been a minister since he was
> baptising a number of people. She drew close to the action
> and listened to the words of the preacher and the singing
> of the riparian congregation. She was so moved that she
> responded to the message and was herself baptised.

The youngest son of her master, Timothy, was awarded a doctorate in theology at Oxford University and spent most of his adult life as a missionary in China. He took on a Chinese identity, changed his name, and founded a national newspaper in China, *The Times*, which was targeted at Chinese intellectuals. Timothy Richard sought greater understanding between Christianity and Buddhism and was a pacifist. This was the radical, nonconformist atmosphere that influenced Margaret and which she communicated to her grandson John.

She was also an eyewitness of the Rebecca riots, where famers and agricultural workers dressed up as women in traditional Welsh costume (as seen in *Salem*) and attacked toll gates in protest against unfair taxation:

> *She remembered seeing torch lights flaming into the dark night and the sons of Rebecca setting fire to toll booths. She also recalled the pursuit of the police and the anxious investigations and prosecutions that took place. Many men were sentenced to life imprisonment in Botany Bay, never to return to their homeland.*

These gangs became known as *Merched Beca* (Welsh for "Rebecca's Daughters") or merely the *Rebeccas*. The origin of their name is said to be a verse in the Bible, Genesis 24:60: "And they blessed Rebekah and said unto her, Thou *art* our sister, be thou *the mother* of thousands of millions, and let thy seed possess the gate of those which hate them."

Margaret met and then married my father's grandfather, another Thomas, also confusingly called Tom. He came from a farming family and the young couple lived for a while in their farm at Ffrwd Val before moving to Ystalyfera in the Swansea Valley, where a large tin and iron works had opened. In search of better, more prominent prospects, they moved again to a little village on the outskirts of Swansea.

My father remembered the day they left Ystalyfera for Gorseinon:

It was in 1886 and they had loaded all their belongings onto a cart and then this family of seven, five children and parents, sat on top of the furniture. On the outskirts of Gorseinon, they had to pass through the river Lliw as there was no bridge there at that time. The tidal river was in full flood and half way across the rear axle snapped and a wheel came off. The cart tilted, tipping some of its human and other cargo. Somehow they made it to their new home in one piece but it was an inauspicious start to their new life.

Margaret's most memorable impact on her grandson's life involved alcohol:

When I was three, my parents went out to a church meeting, leaving me in the care of my grandmother. I'm not sure what happened but by the time they arrived home I was drunk! My dad made his own wine and I think my grandmother mistook it for grape juice.

This is a savage irony, given that John championed the virtues of teetotalism for the rest of his life.

I can see Margaret's values cradled clearly in my father's life. Strong family ties, social justice for the poor, and the necessity of personal faith formed the core of his personality. But his pacifist convictions came from a closer source.

Dad's mother, Martha, was a quiet, demure character, whose life was spent in never-ending domestic exhaustion, caused by the daily round of cleaning the house from industrial dirt brought in from my grandfather's tin plate works and preparing meals on his meagre wage. Even though she was physically weak throughout her life, she inculcated a series of strong principles into her only son, especially an abhorrence of war, indeed of any unnecessary killing. One of Mattie's favourite books was *Uncle Tom's Cabin*, written by American author Harriet Beecher Stowe, which features an array of stoic and determined women who rise above their white and male oppressors.

It was a publishing sensation. After it appeared in 1852, more than 300,000 copies were sold in the USA, whilst in Britain more than a million copies were bought. Next to the Bible, it was the biggest-selling book of the century, occupying a place next to the Bible and *The Pilgrim's Progress* on many shelves.

The gross injustice of slavery; the way in which the life of the black people was worth less than their white counterparts made a deep impression on me. Here was a man whose faith enabled him to transcend the direst of circumstances and here was a home life full of warmth and love.

Uncle Tom's Cabin is credited with fuelling the abolitionist cause in America and playing a part in the events that led to the Civil War. A probably apocryphal story says that when President Abraham Lincoln met Harriet Beecher Stowe, he said: "So this is the little lady who started this Great War."

My mother was frail all the days of her life and not given to great emotion but she loved this novel. I must have only been about six or seven years of age when she said to me, in Welsh, "John, this is the way we must live in this world; loving the Lord Jesus and taking care not to harm the people he has made. We have to try and love everyone, John bach, every life is precious and every soul is precious" [bach is the Welsh for "little" and used as a term of endearment].

One of my most vivid memories is of my mother and father reading to us from Uncle Tom's Cabin. *This must have been when I was very young since the setting is Loughor Common and not Brynhyfryd Road. They took it in turn to read it to us as we huddled around the coal fire, the room lit only by its flames and an oil lamp next to Dat's chair. It was a most gripping story, full of injustice, love and heroism. Dat in particular would get very emotional as he read it. From time to time he would exclaim, "Poor old Tom, poor old Tom." Both my parents would shed a tear at the descriptions of poverty and slavery described by the author.*

Their favourite chapter was called An Evening in Uncle Tom's Cabin. There was something about this description of a poor man's dwelling that really resonated with them but especially the account of a prayer meeting that takes place in this modest place.

… After a while the singing commenced, to the evident delight of all present. Not even all the disadvantage of nasal intonation could prevent the effect of the naturally fine voices, in airs at once wild and spirited. The words were sometimes the well-known and common hymns sung in the churches about, and sometimes of a wilder, more indefinite character, picked up at camp-meetings.

The chorus of one of them, which ran as follows, was sung with great energy and unction:

"Die on the field of battle,
Die on the field of battle,
Glory in my soul."

… Uncle Tom was a sort of patriarch in religious matters,
in the neighbourhood. Having, naturally, an organization
in which the morale was strongly predominant, together
with a greater breadth and cultivation of mind than
obtained among his companions, he was looked up to
with great respect, as a sort of minister among them; and
the simple, hearty, sincere style of his exhortations might
have edified even better educated persons. But it was in
prayer that he especially excelled. Nothing could exceed
the touching simplicity, the child-like earnestness, of his
prayer, enriched with the language of Scripture, which
seemed so entirely to have wrought itself into his being,
as to have become a part of himself, and to drop from his
lips unconsciously; in the language of a pious old negro,
he "prayed right up." And so much did his prayer always
work on the devotional feelings of his audiences, that there
seemed often a danger that it would be lost altogether
in the abundance of the responses which broke out
everywhere around him.[1]

In his later years, my father could become very emotional when
talking about his own parents and the values they passed on to
their children:

*As far as warfare was concerned, Mattie believed it was
a Christian's ethical duty not to fight and take part in an
activity so alien to God's order. With horror she spoke of*

stories she had heard from the Boer war, where British troops had used concentration camps as an instrument of control.

She was one of the most timid people I've ever known and I have no recollection of her ever speaking harshly to anyone; even to her children when they probably deserved it! But she was clear about the sanctity of all life. For her this meant that war was always wrong, as was capital punishment and any kind of oppression. If she'd had the opportunity I think she probably would have been a vegetarian, so strongly did she feel about not taking the life of another of God's creatures. As far as forming my views on pacifism, my mother's voice was the most influential.

CHAPTER 5

Hovel Fit for a King

The reclining chair was invented in France around 1850 and served as a chair, camp bed, and chaise longue. Louis-Napoléon Bonaparte (1808–73), sometimes known as Napoleon III, was reportedly the first owner of this latest trend in home furnishings. The less regal reclining chair now situated in my sister Elizabeth's front room was manufactured in Indiana sometime during the 1930s. It is sturdy and cushioned, although not very comfortable, due largely to its reclining capacity. When the long back of the chair is pushed, it extends into a horizontal single bed, and to my child's eye this gave the chair a "slippy" character. At the time of its manufacture, it would have been regarded as a superior piece of furniture in the UK, unlike the hard wooden chairs normally seen in working-class homes. Domestic comfort was beyond the means of most families more used to flagstone or even mud floors. Houses were poorly heated and ventilated and, more often than not, were overcrowded, with several generations of the same family occupying the same cramped space.

This chair was a gift from my father's uncle, David Theophilus Jones, known as Uncle Davy. Davy emigrated to Gary, Indiana, after World War One and by the time he made his one and only visit home in 1933, he was married with a daughter and had become a manager in the town's largest steel mill. My father remembered the visit for several reasons, particularly for the emotion generated at home. Davy's mother, Margaret, had all but given up on seeing her son again and for the whole of his visit she was either tearful at the thought of his absence or laughing at the pleasure of his presence. But he also brought with him some substantial gifts. These included an expensive Crombie overcoat for Dat, a gold watch for my father, and a reclining chair for the household to enjoy. It must have seemed like an incongruous luxury in Mam and Dat's house compared to the other threadbare furniture. My siblings refer to it as Dat's chair, and this is where our grandfather sat, smoking his pipe or rolling his tobacco next to the open fire after a gruelling ten-hour shift in the rolling mill. Dat gifted the coat to my dad and he wore it until the early 1950s when he bequeathed it to a passing tramp when they were living in Risca, Monmouthshire. The gold watch now resides with my oldest brother David in New Zealand, who was named after Uncle Davy.

Dad's father, my paternal grandfather, Thomas Jones was born in Ystalyfera in the Swansea Valley in 1880, one of five children to Thomas Jones senior and his wife Margaret. Thomas senior had known erratic employment as an agricultural labourer and tin plate worker, and in 1886, as we have seen, the family moved south to Gorseinon, in pursuit of work in the newly opened and burgeoning Grovesend Tin Plate works. South Wales was the new Wild West of the Industrial Revolution and tens of thousands were pouring into the new hotspots of Swansea and the valleys. Like many others across Wales and beyond, this family was escaping from crippling rural poverty in search of industrialization's golden pavements.

Situated on the banks of the River Lliw, the tiny hamlet of Gorseinon was being transformed by the might of industry. This is how local diarist D. Tom Davies describes the scene in the 1880s:

> The introduction of industry meant the influx of workers into the area and the necessity of housing them. The old hamlet was gradually being swallowed up by the village. Mill Street, High Street and Railway Terrace were extended, whilst other streets followed with further industrial development. Most of these were constructed by Messrs. William Lewis & Sons at their own expense upon the lands which they had acquired from the Cameron Estates.
>
> Gorseinon's prosperity was short-lived, for, in 1891 a recession occurred in the tinplate industry when the McKinley Tariff imposed an embargo on the importation of tinplate into the USA. In 1894 the mass unemployment caused by this tariff forced the mill men to share the amount of work available by agreeing to limit their output to 36 boxes per mill, per shift. Such a move was resisted by a few manufacturers who were better-placed in the matter of orders.
>
> Disputes between management and workers developed into a long, drawn-out strike which lasted for seven months and led to the break up, through lack of funds, of the union known as "Undeb Twm Phill".
>
> It was during this strike that the Riot Act was first read in Gorseinon and baton charges were made by the police on the workers. The prelude to the incident was the introduction of "Blacklegs" by the tinplate manufacturers. Men from neighbouring Pontarddulais came along to try

and impede the introduction of such blacklegs with the result that they clashed with the local police.[1]

Thomas Jones senior found a manual labouring job in the tin plate works and the family settled in a new home: 8 Loughor Common. This would be the family's home for two generations, paying inflated rents to a capricious landlord who collected his money every week without fail. The vision of building a better, more prosperous life began in what my father called a "hovel" on the edge of town:

This is where my grandparents lived, then my own parents and my siblings. It was a three up, two down terraced house with no running water and the most primitive of amenities.

Thomas and Margaret's youngest son, Tom, had a very brief school career before finding employment in the tin works at about the age of twelve. However, he took some pride in one of his fellow classmates, as Dad related:

He had grown up with Evan Roberts, the great revivalist who so powerfully influenced the 1904 revival. They went to the same primary school in Loughor and had the same kind of upbringing. Dad went to the tin plate works and Evan went on to work in the mines.

Tom married Martha Eaton Russell in 1906; she was a seamstress from Penclawdd on the Gower Peninsula but had found work "in service" in the area. After their wedding, Tom and Mattie settled in their own home in the town. In 1917, after his father's death, the couple moved:

*In 1917, my parents and two older sisters, Madge and
Nancy, moved in with my widowed grandmother in Loughor
Common. I was born in that house a year later and a few
years later my youngest sister Ceinwen joined us. Looking
back I don't know how we did it. My parents slept in the back
bedroom, my grandmother in the small front bedroom and
my three sisters and I in the slightly larger middle bedroom.
There was no side entrance so everything came in through
the front door. Lime, manure for the garden and coal all had
to be carried down the passage, through the living room and
the kitchen and then into the garden. My poor mother slaved
away each day to scrub the flagstone floors of the house.
These stones sat on top of earth, so there was a constant need
to clean and all in a pervasive atmosphere of damp. Mind
you, Mam was houseproud and everything was spotless.
As far as she was concerned this was no hovel but a king's
palace! If the reigning monarch were to drop by Loughor
Common she didn't wish to be found wanting in her tidyness.
There was no running water in the house; all we had was
a solitary cold water tap outside the back door. Every drop
of water had to be boiled, whether for drinking, washing
dishes and clothes and of course bathing. We had our baths
in a large tin tub in front of the large coal fire in the living
room. My youngest sister Ceinwen and I shared a bath but
everyone else had their own. Poor things, looking back on
it all, they must have done it late at night because there
were always people coming in and out of that living room.
Bathing for Dat was a daily necessity of course as he returned
home from his shift drenched in sweat, oil and the dirt of the
foundry. My poor mother worked herself to the bone keeping
the home as clean as she could and feeding a large family*

on very meagre resources. But she worked her own miracles on a daily basis. She would often buy a sheep's head in the market and somehow managed to make an endless variety of meals for us. We feasted on brawn, soup, and a peculiar Welsh delicacy called Cawl. I particularly loved the occasions when she brought a lamb's stomach home and fed us tripe and onions. We were well nourished despite the difficulties of the period.

These were hard days for Britain, Europe, and the USA. The Great War had depleted stocks of steel, coal, and tin across the world and the high rate of war deaths had resulted in a shortage of skilled labour. Despite this shortage, mine owners decided to cut wages by 13 per cent and boost productivity through longer shifts. This led to a bitter quarrel that eventually blossomed into the General Strike, coordinated by the Trades Union Congress (TUC). On 4 May 1926, one and a half million workers went on strike in support of the miners, including Dat. Fearing civil unrest, the government recruited more than 200,000 special policemen to keep the strikers in order, and the armed forces were also poised to intervene. Tanks were seen in central London and the Royal Navy deployed a battleship off the coast of Newcastle. Buses were set alight in major cities and there were reports of fights between police and strikers. To the embarrassment of the TUC, trade unionists in Russia sent a large donation to their comrades in Britain and the gift was returned, in a bid to dampen accusations of Bolshevism creeping in by the back door. The momentum of dissent continued to increase during the week and striking workers in Northumberland derailed the train, the *Flying Scotsman*, en route to London, leading Prime Minister Stanley Baldwin to announce that Britain was under the threat of revolution. Nearly 400 communists were arrested. Unbeknown to the striking unionists, the head of the TUC, J. H. Thomas, had been in secret talks with the mine owners, and within nine days the other workers drifted back to work, leaving the miners to carry on alone, having achieved nothing.

There was a great strike in 1921 and then again in 1926, and my father was laid off work for weeks on end. I remember him leaving the house early in the morning to collect small pieces of coal from wherever he could find them and returning later to make a fire. He had to supplement the coal with bits of old damp cement which he mixed in with the fuel and tried to dry them before lighting the fire.

Once filled with men in search of employment, the roads of South Wales witnessed an endless procession of beggars and tramps, victims of economic policies made far away in London and Europe and whose brutal reality was felt all too keenly in the working-class areas of Britain. Not yet ten years of age, it was this decade that laid the foundations of my father's political consciousness. Like many others in South Wales at the time, my dad's family lurched from one economic crisis to the next. Industry was still paying heavily for the cost of the First World War and the country was awash with men looking for work.

Mam and Dat never had enough money but somehow they managed to feed a family of four children as well as my grandmother and themselves. Each week Dat would bring home his wages and give them to Mam; she in turn allocated the money to a variety of jars. One was for housekeeping, another for rent and another for the church. But there was another jar which fascinated me. The money in this jar was allowed to accumulate and wasn't spent every week. To start with I thought it was some kind of savings scheme, but this observation turned out to be misplaced. This was for "God's visitors" as Mam called them.

In the 1920s, the roads around Gorseinon and Swansea were regularly filled with men from all over Britain looking for work. Strangely enough, there seemed to be large numbers of men from Brittany selling onions. These were draped all over their bicycles and they would peddle their vegetables around the neighbourhood. We called them Sioni Winwns (Johnny Onions) and they spoke a language very similar to our own. In fact I recall conversations where they spoke Breton to Mam and she replied in Welsh and they all understood each other. But there were many other men who were completely abject and had nothing to sell apart from their labour. I can see them now; threadbare clothes, ragged and broken shoes. They had probably heard of the mines and iron works in the area and came in search of employment. More often than not they were disappointed and sent on their way, told that the company wasn't hiring at that moment. They would then often go from door to door, asking for food. Several times I remember Mam going to that pot and giving them money, as well as giving them food, which she could hardly afford to give. Once someone called at tea time and Mam gave what was on her plate and then went without herself.

I asked her once why she did this and she had several reasons. Jesus was a man of the road and surely we would have looked after him. She also hoped that should the worst come to us as a family we would meet the same kindness in *strangers. And my parents were no different to many others. It was the culture of the area; there was a strong collective sense, of looking out for others. It was Christian communism; an unspoken duty to do unto others as you would have them do unto you.*

The young John was profoundly impacted by the turbulent 1920s with its mixture of post-war gloom, industrial depression, and communal strength:

Even as a boy, I sided with the people and not the powers that governed us. I saw my dear father struggling to provide for us and there were many like him in Gorseinon. Men who wanted to work hard but were thwarted by decisions made far away in London. I remember hearing of a friend's father being fined heavily for taking coal from a nearby pit and it brought ruin on the family and I felt so angry. He had to go before the magistrates' court and his name was soiled publicly even though he was only trying to provide for his own. But I also saw how my parents and our neighbours pulled together and supported that family. We all had so little and yet no one was left to suffer on their own. I didn't understand what was going on in the local mines and works but I knew that you couldn't trust the important people who made the big decisions but you should always believe in the power of working people supporting each other.

Despite it all, there was some light in the darkness. In 1926 the inhabitants of 8 Loughor Common were rehoused in a new council house in Brynhyfryd Road, in the centre of Gorseinon.

It seemed like heaven to us and everything changed completely straight away, as far as home life was concerned anyway. We had electricity for the first time and didn't have to rely on candles or gas lamps or smelly paraffin heaters. And there was an indoor toilet and a bathroom with piping hot water available all the time! We were surrounded by large families and I felt we had moved to paradise. Directly opposite where we lived was the Liske family and I became great friends with one of their sons, Glyn. He became a constant companion, but things turned out for the worse for them all. Mr Liske had to give up his work as a miner due to coal dust on his lungs and he died soon afterwards. The family was given permission to collect small coal from the pit every morning, so Glyn would walk there before school, come home and then make the fire and then go to school without any breakfast. I remember him fainting with exhaustion several times before lunchtime. He was a really bright boy but he didn't have a chance with all the burdens he had to bear.

In 1933 Dat suffered a near-crippling industrial accident which laid him off work for months. He worked in the rolling mill of the tin plate works, the hottest and most dangerous part of the plant. Large sheets of white-hot tin would roll off the mill and his work was to catch, lift, and stack them before they hit the floor.

It was dangerous work and required intense concentration for hours on end. These sheets were hot from the furnace and came at him at great speed. I remember him coming home completely drained after a day's shift. One day as he handled the tin plate, the extreme heat tore through his gloves, and sparks shot into his eyes, leaving him blind in one eye. He

was laid off work for months on end; it was initially feared
that he might even die. It was a period of great anxiety for
my mother especially. To make matters worse, company
bosses told him that if he made a complaint against them, his
wages would be cut immediately.

Sick payments only lasted a matter of weeks and the family would have been thrown into desperate poverty, had it not been for the steel workers' union that Dat had helped to form. The British Steel Smelters' Amalgamated Association had a scheme in place to financially support men unable to work through ill health and this small amount was the difference between survival and ruin for Dat and his family.

In his 1983 diary John's sense of belonging and identity is clearly shown coming from his parents' working-class culture. A documentary programme on BBC TV Wales (first shown in 1961) stimulated his own memory:

Two old men who had left their jobs on Cardiganshire
farms for richer pickings in the Rhondda mines at the start
of the century, sat on a bench in a valley street, talking
naturally and freely as though there were no television
camera in sight. Aided by very fine camera work – in black
and white of course – of reading rooms and libraries in
Workmen's Halls, the whole programme was a powerful
evocation of a Rhondda – and indeed a Wales – that has
largely disappeared. The differing beliefs of the two old
men – the one a humanist who believed that a man-made
utopia was just around the corner and the other a Christian
whose firm conviction that in Christ alone was the hope of
a better world. Their native wit and facility in arguing their

case, their grasp of literature and ease with one another, all conspired to give a picture of a cultured, dignified, articulate working class in which I am proud to have my roots.

Although he never worked in a mine or foundry, my father throughout his days identified himself as working class, in no small measure due to his father's influence.

Dat was a hard drinking tin plate worker. The shifts were long, hard and often dangerous; these men were labouring in intense heat, handling huge and fast moving sheets of tin under great pressure. And they sweated so much and lost so much salt that going to the public house and drinking beer was part of the working day. You need to understand that they were thirsty and often weakened by this daily ordeal. Dat was a self taught man, he could read Greek and Latin, and he said to me on several occasions that working in the foundry was like a scene from Dante's inferno.

Even though we went to chapel as a family, it never meant a great deal to Dat. He came along with Mam and us children, but that was true of every man and his family. It was the way of things in those days. But he changed after the accident and one Saturday he went to Aberavon on the train to hear a gifted young preacher called Dr Martyn Lloyd Jones. This man had given up a career as a Harley Street psychiatrist and was making quite a name for himself as a minister in the Sandfields area of the town. After hearing the young preacher, Dat was a changed man. He came home that night and said "Today I've heard a message that's cut right through me. I thought that living a good life was enough but that young man has shown me I need the power of God to give me new life."

Out of his pockets he took his pipe and tobacco and placed them in the fire. He told my mother and the children who were present that he wanted to be an example to his family and especially his only son and that from that day onwards he would never smoke or drink alcohol again. And as far as I can remember, he never did, even though there must have been plenty of reasons for him to go back on his pledge.

The wooden reclining chair, now in my oldest sister's house, is also testimony to a difference of opinion between father and son. During the Great War, Dat worked in a munitions factory in Southampton, although his ambitions lay elsewhere.

Southampton was a bitter sweet period for Dat. He had tried to enlist as a soldier but was refused on the grounds that he was involved in an exempt trade. The war effort needed huge supplies of steel and tin, and my father was relocated to Southampton to work in the shipyards. It was always a source of disappointment to him that he couldn't fight for king and country.

This surprised me, and this quiet man who died in the year of my birth was full of them. Not only did he take part in the Great War, but as the war grew more intense in 1917, he attempted to travel to Russia to fight alongside the Bolsheviks. He was a complex individual: backing king and empire against the Kaiser, standing shoulder to shoulder with Lenin.

CHAPTER 6

I Was in School with Him

I am looking at a black and white class photograph taken of a secondary school year in 1933. Behind the pupils is a red-brick wall with two classroom windows, one of which is open. Sitting in the centre of the middle row is a bespectacled male form tutor, cross-armed and sporting an academic gown, a pencil moustache, and a smug grin. The form is co-educational with fifteen girls and fourteen boys, and there is a great variation in their physical development. Some of the children look older than their master whilst others look considerably younger and smaller than their peers. About four of them must have fidgeted or moved just as the photographer took his shot since their faces are blurred. They are all about to sit their elementary exams, the next rung on the academic ladder after successfully passing their entrance examination four years earlier. If successful, they will stay on at school and matriculate in two years' time. The matriculation exam is essential for entrance to higher education. The girls' uniform is a dark pinafore-style frock with white shirt, and some of them are wearing ties. The boys are wearing a range of light and dark jackets, complete with ties and some pullovers. My father is third from the right on the back row, and is the second-tallest boy in the group (all the girls are seated on chairs or the floor). His expression is determined with a faint smile and he is wearing a blazer buttoned tightly over a patterned pullover. On his left lapel is a badge.

My father was a pupil at Gowerton County Intermediate School from 1929 to 1935. The Welsh Intermediate Education Act became law on 5 March 1898, "to make further provision for the intermediate and technical education of the inhabitants of Wales and the county of Monmouth". The school opened on 5 March 1898, initially to educate boys, becoming co-educational later. The intention of the intermediate school system was to provide a high-quality technical education, although many of the schools emulated the more established public and grammar schools in their curriculum. Latin, English, Algebra, and Science were staple subjects in Gowerton, with the vast majority of the pupils going on to universities in Wales and England. My father always referred to his school as Gowerton Grammar School, although it only officially became known as this after the 1944 Education Act.

Enrolment at the school was only possible through passing an entrance examination. Successful candidates received a state-funded education with the prospect of higher education for able pupils who matriculated at the age of eighteen.

I don't think I appreciated at the time how lucky I was to gain a place in that school. In the final year of primary school I was part of a small group that was coached for the entrance examination. My health wasn't terribly good at the time on the day of the exam. I felt poorly but my mother ensured I went to school to take it. No one was more surprised than I was to pass the thing! And from the first day I felt I had

entered a new, grown up world. The headmaster, D.E. "Boss"
Williams, was an imposing man and swept around the school
in his long black gown. In fact all the masters wore gowns
and quite a few had been to either Oxford or Cambridge
University.

Throughout his life, John remained a very proud alumnus of his school. He often regaled us with tales of peers who had achieved some greatness in public life. Whether it was the composers Alun Hoddinott and Karl Jenkins or the writer and broadcaster Sir Alun Talfan Davies, he basked in vicarious glory. He was particularly vocal about Gowerton's rugby-playing prowess, be it the modern-day boy wonders of Liam Williams and Dan Biggar, or players from his own generation. Among them were two sporting cousins, Haydn Tanner and Willie Davies. Although only teenagers and still in sixth form, these boys played club rugby for Swansea RFC and went on to gain caps for Wales and the British and Irish Lions. Their finest moment came on 28 September 1935 when they represented Swansea against the mighty New Zealand All Blacks. It was a stunning victory for Swansea, defeating New Zealand by eleven points to three. It was the first time ever that a club side had beaten a full touring New Zealand team. Played in wet and windy conditions at St Helens with frequent fighting amongst the forwards, the influence of Haydn at scrum half and Willie at outside half was pivotal to the victory. Such was their contribution, it led the Kiwis' captain, Jack Manchester, to comment: "Tell them back home we were beaten by all means, but please, not by a couple of school kids."[1]

Whenever a former student appeared on television or radio, my father generally exclaimed, "I was in school with him." During my teenage years it seemed that most of the people on television must have been educated in Gowerton Grammar School.

Curiously enough, even though none of the staff spoke Welsh,
we were allowed to speak it as pupils, a right not afforded
to us in primary school. I wasn't by any means the brightest
student in my form but I made good progress and worked
hard. The expectations on us were high; not only did the
masters tell us that hard work would be rewarded with great
prospects but my parents repeated the same sentiments. As
the only boy in the family, they wanted me to do my best for
the whole family. Mind you I enjoyed every aspect of school.
Learning, drama, and sport – it remained and still remains
to me a special time in my life.

Beyond the sleepy industrial confines of Gorseinon, as my father's career in the school continued, there was increasing unease at developments in Germany. In 1933, Adolf Hitler's National Socialist (Nazi) party swept into power in Germany with Hitler becoming Chancellor. His vision was to restore the greatness and borders of the fatherland, particularly after the crushing limitations imposed by the Treaty of Versailles after the First World War. From 1935 onwards, he began an extensive rearmament programme and conscription was introduced. In March 1936, Chancellor Hitler ordered his armed forces to seize the Rhineland, a demilitarized zone since 1919. He also entered into the Rome–Berlin Axis with Italy's Mussolini and signed the Anti-Comintern Pact with Japan, in opposition to the Third International, a movement which promoted world communism. Under the terms of this pact, if one of the parties entered into war against the Soviet Union, the others would take supportive measures. By 1937, Germany, Italy, and Japan had withdrawn from the League of Nations, an increasingly fragile institution established after the First World War to guard against another global conflict. The momentum seemed to be with these three countries, particularly after the 1934 World Disarmament Conference failed to reach an international arms limitation agreement. Germany withdrew from the conference and Italian forces marched into Abyssinia (now Ethiopia) in 1935, making it part of the new Italian empire. In Spain, republicans rose up against General Franco's nationalist forces in 1936 but failed to remove him from power.

A number of local men went out to fight for the republicans in Spain. It was seen as an internationalist battle between ordinary working people and the forces of fascism. It exercised Dat greatly and at one point he was talking seriously about going out there himself. My mother pointed out however that he would be of no great use to them with his weak hands and dodgy back! But as a trade union leader, my father felt this great affinity with his comrades in Spain and he said that many Welshmen were fighting in newly formed trade union brigades against Franco's forces.

Gorseinon also had its fair share of veterans from the Great War: ageing men with unsightly scars, or fumbling with clunky prosthetic limbs. There were men in the district who were seen as being unhinged or dangerous because they spoke only to themselves, rambling on and on about the soundscape of Ypres. But the most feared were the ones who said nothing at all, locked into a mute hell from which there was no escape.

Dad remembered one of his masters who taught Mathematics:

The poor man was the most temperamental teacher I'd ever had. He clearly wasn't well, as there were extended periods when he was absent from school. He'd served as a junior officer and seen action in the Battle of the Somme. He was forever trying to clear his chest and was a heavy smoker. His eyesight was poor and he had a constant tremor in his hands. The man was brilliant apparently, had a double first from Oxford, but by the time he came to Gorseinon he was a nervous wreck. He was a real loner and the gown draped over his slumped shoulders gave him a funereal air. Some of the boys in the area were very unkind to him, standing outside his house and hearing him crying and muttering to himself.

By and large, the British government's attitude was to maintain a neutral position as Germany stocked up and its democratic institutions were destroyed. It wasn't Britain's business, best to keep out of it. Arm's-length diplomacy was the way forward. This bent towards peace through negotiation was seen ten days after Hitler came to power in 1933, when the Oxford University Union debated the motion "That this House will in no circumstances fight for its King and country". A similar motion had been debated in the Cambridge University Union in 1927 when Arthur Ponsonby proposed "That lasting peace can only be secured by the people of England adopting an uncompromising attitude of pacifism". It was passed by 213 votes to 138.

The Oxford debate was heated and at times acrimonious, and generated considerable and largely negative media coverage, unlike its predecessor, which appears to have had no media coverage at all. Among others, Quintin Hogg, later a leading MP, spoke against the motion and the philosopher C. E. M. Joad spoke in support; a disappointment since it had been hoped that Bertrand Russell would lead the charge for the pacifists. Joad's delivery however was powerfully persuasive and he won the day.

On 17 February 1933, in a speech to the Anti-Socialist and Anti-Communist Union, Winston Churchill condemned the motion:

> My mind turns [to] where great nations stand determined to defend their national glories or national existence.... I think of Germany, with its splendid clear-eyed youth... burning to suffer and die for their fatherland. I think of Italy, with her... stern sense of national duty. I think of France... peace-loving... but armed to the teeth, and determined to survive as a great nation... One can almost feel the curl of contempt upon the lips of the manhood of all these people when they read this message sent out... in the name of young England.[2]

With the wide coverage generated by the "King and Country" debate, it sparked lively discussions beyond Oxford:

> *I read the news reports about the debate and it created quite a stir in school. I remember having discussions with my friends about it all and there were times when the masters joined in. Quite a few of them had fought in the First World War and they declared themselves to be of a pacifist persuasion. Even before war broke out there was a real hope that war could be avoided and Hitler appeased. It was at this time that my own anti-war convictions crystallised as I recall. I was so vocal in my opposition to warfare in general that I was asked to speak in favour of pacifism in a form debate. The motion under consideration went along the lines of:*
> *"This form believes that it is the nation's duty not to fight against aggressive neighbours."*

*It was all very formal; our form master was the chairman
and I spoke in favour of the motion and someone else spoke
against it and then the boys voted on the matter. I won the
debate, which was very satisfying.*

This period, and 1933 in particular, as we shall see later, proved
to be a turning point in my father's intellectual and personal
development. The 1926 General Strike had left him with a deep
mistrust of government and big business. This, combined with
Dat's recent industrial accident, confirmed to John that ordinary
people were used and abused by powers beyond their control. But
he also witnessed the collective support and protest of the union,
the kindness of his local community, and the message of hope
preached in the family's chapel.

*We worshipped in Noddfa, a small mission chapel in the
village. A generation earlier, work had begun on a much
larger building to house the anticipated numbers that might
attend. Funds ran out however and the people stayed in the
small building in the shadow of the half built fantasy. My
father was a Sunday school teacher and I had been going
there since I was a baby. Our social life revolved around
the chapel with its choir, dramatic society and Band of
Hope, a youth club based on the principles of temperance.
The minister was a very bright man and a fine preacher;
although he was also a delicate and sickly soul. Radical
in theology and politics alike, he espoused what he called
Christian communism and argued that Marxism could be
seen in the way the early church organised itself. He was also
an outspoken pacifist and he had this knack of finding non-
violent protest wherever he looked in the Bible. He got very*

excitable in the pulpit and would sometimes go into what we
called the "hwyl", a kind of ecstatic state where the preacher
seemed to sing the sermon in a highly emotional way. It was
through him that I began my lifelong love of reading.

And read he did. From the age of thirteen, John explored the
authors cited by his minister:

There was a public lending library in the village and also
the working men's hall had a magnificent stock of books.
People find it hard to believe, but there were daily evening
lectures on everything from philosophy to art, right through
to learning classical languages. My father barely had an
education but he could hold his own in any discussion about
history or current affairs.

Through the writings of Mohandas Gandhi and a
Japanese writer called Toyohiko Kagawa, I discovered the
power of non-violent protest. Gandhi's refusal to accept
English rule in India through dialogue and fasting was
inspirational to me. Here was a man who knew his own
mind but whose principles forbade the shedding of human
blood. I'd also discovered the works of the Danish philosopher
Søren Kierkegaard, who saw Christianity as an inner reality,
beyond the confines of language and form, and was scathing
against institutional religion.

My father's classroom oratory brought him to the attention of a
local literary society, The Cymrodorion. This group was part of
a movement that traced its origins back to London in the early
1700s. Set up to support the thousands of Welsh people pouring
into the capital, it also sought to promote Welsh literature and

culture by means of wealthy benefactors. The organization went through considerable change but eventually sponsored the national Eisteddfod, the National Library of Wales, and encouraged local societies to be formed throughout the nation.

I was invited to give a presentation by my form master, who had heard me debate a few weeks earlier. He asked me to give my defence of pacifism but this time there would be no motion or debate. I felt honoured to be asked, especially when he told me that I was the youngest speaker they'd ever had.

It was held in a church hall and the room was packed with adults. I felt very nervous but my teacher was very encouraging and told me to take my time and speak clearly. It was a strange sort of meeting. It wasn't religious as such, although it was very formal, and there were a few times when people recited certain pledges in Welsh. We even sang the national anthem at the beginning. By the time I got to my feet, I was trembling and perspiring. As I looked out across the crowded room I recognised a number of people immediately. My minister was smiling at me and a number of school teachers stared back at me, their faces like shovels. I also saw a few shop owners, our doctor, several church ministers and our MP.

I started by referring to the Oxford Union's King and Country debate, arguing that there was no mood in the country for another war and that people had lost faith in politicians who seemed to represent their own interests instead of the people who voted for them. Surprisingly enough, this seemed to go down well with the MP.

I then went on to talk about the basis of my pacifism, namely that warfare was totally incompatible with the

*teachings of Jesus Christ. His command, as I saw it, was
that we should love and not kill each other. As far as I was
concerned this was an absolute requirement of his followers
and not one that could be changed by nation states picking a
fight with other countries and making it compulsory for their
citizens to fight and kill each other. I quoted extensively from
Gandhi's books and also Kagawa. I paid particular attention
to his Kingdom of God movement which called Christians to
work for justice and equality in the world's poor areas and
work against state sponsored greed, including war.*

*At the end of my speech I received a polite although
not rapturous applause. The MP whom I thought I had
impressed left without saying a word to me. My church
minister was very enthusiastic and was clearly moved that
I had cited the writers and thinkers that he regarded highly.
He even told me I possessed the gifts to become a preacher
and that I should seriously think about church ministry.*

There was however a member of the audience unknown to my
father, but highly influential in the district. His name was Mr
Thomas and he was a senior manager in the Grovesend Tin works
where Dat worked.

*He asked after my father, said he'd heard about the accident
and asked me to pass on his best wishes for a speedy recovery.
I thought to myself, "It's your company that's allowed this to
happen and you've done nothing about it." But I remained
silent. But instead of leaving, he started a conversation; or
rather it was a monologue. He accused me of being idealistic
and naive. It was all well and good having good morals and
a proper regard for God, but what the world needed was*

men of action and not belief. If the "hun", as he called the Germans, attacked again, it was every man's duty to protect their family and community. He told me that war would be good news for the tin works, for my father even, because it would be Welsh industry driving the war effort, thus ensuring full employment. And if I had any sense of ambition for my life I would do better thinking more practically about the way things are rather than chasing a schoolboy dream.

To my shame I said nothing. I felt intimidated, rather in awe of him. He seemed so powerful and respectable compared to me a mere schoolboy. He was confident, influential and I came from a very modest home. More than that, I was looking at the man who employed my dad and I knew how vital it was for my father to keep his job. There was much I wanted to say and I couldn't. In that moment I thought of my mother and how she so impressed on us as children that we should always be polite and never drop our guard.

Caught in that moment, that's how I remember my father several decades later. A man of great passion and principle and yet strangely timid when confronted by another forcibly expressed position. Voluble at home, impassioned among friends, and yet put him in a pulpit or face him with action, and he turned quiet when it was time for his opinions to be heard.

Not given to joining movements, John heard of a Church of England vicar trying to garner support for pacifism as the nations of the world rattled their sabres in preparation for war. The vicar was the Reverend Dick Sheppard, and he had served as a chaplain in the First World War. This experience had left him with a deep moral objection to war which resulted in endless letters to the press railing against war. He bore mental scars from his wartime experiences and suffered periods of acute depression. In 1933, Sheppard heard of a sermon preached by the New York church minister Harry Emerson Fosdick. During the sermon Fosdick said the following words:

> I renounce war. I renounce war because of what it does
> to our own men… I renounce war because of what it
> compels us to do to our enemies… I renounce war for its
> consequences, for the lies it lives on and propagates, for the
> undying hatreds it arouses, for the dictatorships it puts in
> place of democracy, for the starvation that stalks after it. I
> renounce war and never again, directly or indirectly, will I
> sanction or support another.

So moved was Sheppard that he wrote a letter which *The Times* refused to publish, but which did appear in the *Manchester Guardian* and other papers on 16 October 1934. The letter concluded with the extract from Fosdick's sermon and an invitation to send a postcard to Sheppard signalling willingness to join a public demonstration against war.

John read the article and sent his postcard. And he was not alone. After a few weeks, more than 30,000 replies had been received. This makeshift protest group was initially called the Sheppard Peace Movement and a demonstration was planned to take place in the Albert Hall on 14 July 1935. With the aid of other well-known pacifists such as George Lansbury and Donald Soper, the organization was renamed the Peace Pledge Union. In spite of Sheppard's passionate Christian convictions, the newly constituted movement was deliberately inclusive and open to "men and women of very divergent philosophic, religious and political opinions".[3]

My father didn't make the journey to the Albert Hall, but did receive a badge emblazoned with the inscription PPU which he presumably wore with pride. He was wearing it on his lapel the day the class photograph was taken.

CHAPTER 7

John the Baptist

150 YEARS OLD CAUSE

Third Jubilee of a Baptist Church, near Llandilo

Centenary of the Present Chapel

**Large congregations attended the celebrations at
Bethel Baptist Church, Pontbrenaraeth, near Llandilo,
on Wednesday and Thursday 27th and 28th July, in
connection with the third jubilee of the cause and the
centenary of the present chapel.**

Extract from the Carmarthen Journal, *Friday 5 June 1942*

This is the opening paragraph of a page-long leading article, referring to the founding of a Baptist church in 1792. The newspaper in which the story appeared was founded in 1810 and claims to be the oldest one in Wales. The *Carmarthen Journal* continues to serve the county of Carmarthenshire, a hilly and largely rural area except for a few industrial hotspots on its eastern borders. At the time of this feature article, over 80 per cent of the population spoke Welsh, although according to the 2011 census this has now dropped to 50 per cent of its inhabitants. To the west and north are the counties of Pembrokeshire, Ceredigion, and Powys, whilst the east is dominated by the densely populated former county of Glamorgan, now parcelled into several unitary authorities. The article's author, Revd G. Edmund Williams, was the church's minister in 1942, and a photograph of him is included on the page. Sporting a dog collar and three-piece suit he has striking features. With his slickly combed-back blond hair, blue sunken eyes, aquiline nose, and strong jaw, Mr Williams' portrait exudes a confident, if not oily, personality. He describes in detail the personalities and families that created this chapel in the very small hamlet of Pontbrenaraeth in the mountains of north-east Carmarthenshire.

Bethel Baptist Church was founded by William Morris, a former innkeeper who after his conversion and baptism "proclaimed the Baptist principles" (to quote Revd Williams) and proceeded to advance his new faith in the village. Whereas he had formerly promoted open-air dancing in Pontbrenaraeth, this was now replaced by preaching. Early converts were baptized in the River Araeth, and so great was their number that the particular location of this event was known as "pwll y bedydd", or baptism pool.

After an initial burst of interest and growth, we are told that the church hit a barren patch due to the divisive preaching of a local lay preacher and tailor by the name of Jac Gruffydd. A vivid story cited by the feature writer had also been passed down to my father, who in turn relayed it to his own family:

A good story is related of a local farmer who went to the service, followed by his dog, to hear Jac Gruffydd. He listened attentively for a while, but disapproving of his Unitarian doctrine, he suddenly rose and shouted, "That is not the way to heaven," and calling his dog he walked out in protest.

Despite financial difficulties and decline, matters improved for this small church and in 1842 a new chapel was built and then enlarged in 1872. At the heart of these projects was my great-great-grandfather, Williams Jones "The Lodge". He seems to have been a generous benefactor of the Baptist cause, which suggests a degree of wealth not evident in later generations. The three sons of his only daughter Mary are mentioned, although the identity of their mother is veiled from the reader; she is simply the "mother of three well known ministers". The three siblings and fellow Baptist ministers in question were the Reverends William Samuel Jones of Llwynypia, John Samuel Jones of St David's, and David Samuel Jones of Bridgend. I found this thin and yellowing page of newsprint inside one of my dad's diaries. I remember him talking about the baptisms mentioned in the last paragraph, largely because he used to swim as a young boy in these same waters. In his final few years he often used to talk about Pontbrenaraeth with a faraway look in his eyes; this was a place which gave him a deep nostalgic resonance. Sadly I never paid too much attention to his reminiscences, more aware of his lachrymose emotions than the content of his speech. I know, more fool me. If only I'd listened properly to those tales of childhood summers spent plunging into the clear waters of the River Araeth or memories of bardic competitions that went long into the night. I vaguely remember him talking about local poets vying with each other in complicated Welsh metrical forms as people packed into his great-grandparents William and Anne's dimly lit farmhouse in the Lodge, Pontbrenaraeth.

According to my research, my father's paternal family line surfaced in this small Carmarthenshire hamlet in the mid-1700s. Where they were before that time is anyone's guess as I haven't been able to get beyond that period. I suspect however that they were farm labourers and agricultural workers in north Carmarthenshire.

There are two reasons why this press cutting commands my attention. And in turn two questions have been answered. The first concerns my father's religious affiliation. The church referred to in this cutting is Bethel Baptist Church, celebrating 150 years as a religious community. Up to this point I had assumed that my dad's passionate Baptist faith was something he chose in his teenage years. It turns out he was born into a long line of Christians who prided themselves on independent thought, fiery personal faith, and the complete separation of church and state. It seems to me that the Baptist persuasion chose him and not the other way round; my dad's religious destiny was fixed generations before he was born.

The second question is the identity of the three brothers. Dad often spoke of these three men, referring to them by their initials and surname, particularly W. S. and D. S. Jones. The former had returned from church ministry in Pennsylvania just before the Welsh revival of 1904 and became a prominent figure in that spiritual awakening. According to my father, D. S. was less gifted than his brothers but his passion for social justice and evangelism made a great impact on him.

John's five happy years in Gowerton Intermediate County School came to an abrupt end at the beginning of 1934. His parents' attempts to limp by financially after the long lay-off caused by Dat's industrial accident brought them perilously close to ruin. The only choice left to them was for John to leave school immediately and start work in a clothing firm in nearby Llanelli. In September, at the age of sixteen, John started work at Morris the Realm:

There was only one choice that could be made. Dat's lost income had to be replaced and I was the only one who could earn a wage to support us. Madge and Nancy were now married and Ceinwen was too young to work. I was happy to help out but I was disappointed to leave school. I enjoyed academic work and had been tipped to do well in my Matriculation but I was offered a job by Madge's husband, Vincent, in a shop in Llanelli.

I had done well in my elementary exams but the all-important Matriculation, or Matric as we called it, was ahead of me. Without successfully passing that examination I would have no chance of getting into university, and more than anything, that was my ambition. I had no clear sense of what I wanted to study and even less the shape of any future career or vocation. The only real direction came from my minister, who had repeatedly told me I should consider Baptist church ministry. And I must say I did feel inspired by this prospect. I enjoyed public speaking, and the theology I was reading had given me a new way of looking at the world and the church. In addition, I enjoyed listening to people and trying to understand how they experienced life.

This was a period in Dad's life of great spiritual interest and inquiry. Like more or less everyone else in the village, as we have seen his family were regular churchgoers and their Baptist chapel, Noddfa, played a pivotal role in their social and cultural lives. However, even though his family's experiences of Christianity were neither unusually pious nor zealous, something was happening to John.

Our minister, Rev TB Humphrey, was a real firebrand. He was unlike the other preachers I had heard before; at that time there were still performers filling the pulpits; men whose oratory and delivery gave them the status of celebrity. Personality and "presence" gave them large followings, although their content was often lacking. This man was different, and even though he had the same skills as all the rest, it was his sincere faith that captivated me. He preached Christ as someone to follow and imitate.; of the fatherhood of God, the brotherhood of man and the urgency of building the Kingdom of God on earth. Action and discipleship were more important than doctrine and he had a tendency to be controversial in his messages. His preaching was peppered with references to contemporary scholarship, some of which was political and undermined traditional readings of the Bible. It was through him I heard of Kagawa, Gandhi and Muriel Lester. One Sunday evening he quoted a line penned by Kagawa and it riveted me: "I read a book that a man called Christ went about doing good. It is very disconcerting to me that I am so easily satisfied with just going about." I thought to myself, that's what I want: to know the dynamic presence of Christ and not the empty formalism I see all around me.

Baptists appeared in England in the early seventeenth century, part of the endless schisms of the Protestant Reformation. Its early fathers, John Smyth and Thomas Helwys, established a congregation in Spitalfields, London, and argued for a complete separation of church and state: allowing Christians to determine their own affairs without the intervention of secular rulers. The freedom of conscience in religious matters had to be protected from the control of the state. There were of course many other distinctive beliefs, but this separatist attitude produced churches whose prime allegiance was to God as interpreted in the Bible. Where the government of the day acted in accordance with the teachings of the Bible, Baptists were exhorted to be model citizens. But in instances of conflict, where rulers acted in defiance of their plain understanding of Scripture, Baptists were not reticent in voicing their dissent. Many in their ranks sided with Wilberforce in opposing the slave trade and in later years became vocal trade unionists and socialists. Many Baptist men heeded the call of the king and his government to bear arms in the Great War, but by 1939 many refused to fight. They had, it seemed, lost faith in the political class's intentions.

The first Baptist church in Wales, now in ruins, dates back to 1649 and was founded by an Oxford graduate called John Myles. After graduating from Brasenose College, Myles attended the Glasshouse church in London, an offshoot of the church set up by Smyth and Helwys. He later returned to his homeland and planted a Baptist congregation in Ilston, a small village on the Gower Peninsula, where he stayed until 1663, during which time he also served under Cromwell's government. However, in 1662, the Act of Uniformity was passed compelling every clergyman of every denomination to assent to the Book of Common Prayer and to receive a bishop's ordination. Unwilling to comply and fearing reprisals for his disobedience, Myles fled to Plymouth, Massachusetts, where he served in a Baptist congregation before planting a new congregation in the new town he and other settlers had built: Swansea, Massachusetts.

The Industrial Revolution in Wales was kind towards the Baptists, a denomination based on democratic principles. Members of these churches were expected to attend meetings where collective decisions were made on virtually everything connected to the life of their community. Organizational skills were acquired and honed as people learned to budget, chair meetings, and make arguments which were then voted on by other members. It was a corporate structure familiar to miners, steel and tin workers, many of whom campaigned together for better conditions in their places of work. But these chapels were also rich in dramatic, literary, temperance, and choral societies. More often than not, they were at the heart of everything, and as people poured into the valleys and towns of South Wales in search of work, they found a welcome in these busy and bustling churches.

Even in my father's youth there were hundreds of churches dotted across the country, despite dwindling numbers after World War One. From about the age of fifteen onwards, he developed a serious interest in his faith; not from a historical point of view but through exploring the dominant thinkers of the 1930s. The theological movement that grabbed his attention was known as the Kingdom of God movement, and its proponents believed the time had come to express a more inclusive and loving form of Christianity. Here is how the American Glenn Clark described this movement in 1935:

> The only creed that Jesus laid down as an indispensable
> working faith was God, our Father, all men brothers, and
> Love, the law of Life. He embodied these principles so
> completely in His own life that merely to look at Jesus,
> to follow Him, to open our hearts to Him and to let Him
> enter and possess us, will solve all the problems of our
> lives. As Jesus lived these principles, let us do our best to
> live Jesus.[1]

There was one man whose name my father venerated more than any other: Toyohiko Kagawa. Now largely forgotten, in my dad's youth Kagawa represented a fresh vision of global justice that went hand in hand with evangelism. Born in Kobe, Japan, in 1888, Toyohiko Kagawa's mother was a geisha and his father a wealthy businessman. Before Kagawa reached the age of five, both parents had died and he was taken into the care of American missionaries. At the age of fifteen, he had an experience of Christ's love, and he started to study to be a minister. As a consequence of his understanding of the Gospels and the message of the kingdom of God, he was drawn to live and work in the slums of Kobe, home to 10,000 people living in the most squalid of conditions. Instead of becoming involved as a leader in the church establishment, he created a new order in 1921 called the Society of the Friends of Jesus. Based on the discipleship methods he admired within both Buddhism and the Jesuits, the Friends' purpose was to create ecumenical reform within the church and make the kingdom of God central to its message. Kagawa's vision was to win 1 million Japanese people for Christ by exposing them to the love of God.

Two dominant themes emerged in Kagawa's writings. First was the emphasis he placed on developing a mystical, inner relationship with Christ through prayer. Even though Christ was central to his faith, he was open to divine goodness wherever he found it: in music, art, literature, and even other religions. Secondly was the need to live out the message of Christ practically by championing justice for the poor through non-violent protest against corrupt political structures:

The Kingdom of God is an eternal aspiration after God
and for a program that unfolds forever. It is ever moving

upward and onward toward a perfectly organized and unselfish society.

The goal of the Kingdom of God Movement is a Christian society, the Christianization of every community. It envisages an economic social order where love shall be the dominant motive and the principle of the Cross spontaneously practiced.[2]

The main voice of the Kingdom of God movement in Britain was a woman, Muriel Lester. Born into a wealthy Baptist family, she and her sister lived in the East End of London and established a community where the poorest could come and live. Convinced that the kingdom of God answered humanity's deepest needs, she campaigned against poverty and assumed a leadership role within the International Fellowship of Reconciliation, a pacifist group that successfully lobbied conscientious objectors during the First World War. Like Kagawa, she formed alliances with people of other faiths, including Gandhi, whom my father greatly admired. She also toured Asia with Kagawa and was committed to combating child poverty.

I knew people who'd listened to her preach in Swansea on one of her tours. She always drew a large crowd because of her wide range of interests. She was a passionate preacher, a social worker, had set up a community in the East End by spending all her inheritance and living on nothing and she was a pacifist. And at a time when there was so much fear about another war, she brought hope of a better and purer future. That's what really appealed to me: that we could have a part in building God's Kingdom instead of having to tolerate the power struggles of governments and nations.

Like Kagawa, Lester's emphasis on the kingdom of God led to transformative change in society:

> Once you have found your relationship to God, you need never look around for work. From that moment every person is your friend and your brother. Your job is to build up the Kingdom of God. Here, now, on earth. You find every circumstance and every moment rich in creative opportunity. Even sin, your own and other people's, is found to be a steppingstone to a deeper knowledge, a clearer understanding. Your task is to set up, here and now, wherever you happen to be, the reign of God, the Kingdom of Heaven on Earth.[3]

As Dad settled into his new job at the men's outfitters shop, he found the work interesting, aware that he was learning some valuable lessons:

> *I'd been used to the energy and pace of school life but this was different. I had to learn the art of salesmanship, something with which I was totally unfamiliar. I discovered of course that sales is really about getting alongside people and finding out what makes them tick. Lessons were learnt in that shop that lasted the rest of my life.*

Dad was now actively exploring church ministry as a career and wondering how he would get to university without the necessary qualifications. As part of this exploratory process, he attended Baptist Missionary Society summer schools in Ilston; they involved a mixture of practical work and learning theology. But he was looking for a spiritual experience that seemed to elude him.

In the summer of 1936, I was invited along to some special meetings held in another chapel in Gorseinon. The speaker was a young man by the name of David Shepherd, an itinerant evangelist who was apparently a very gifted speaker. I went along and found his message completely engaging and quite different to anything I'd heard before. There were boys there from my old school and it was so good to see them in this environment. He preached from the book of Romans where it says that all have sinned and fallen short of the glory of God. As he developed his theme of the hopelessness of the human condition without Christ, his manner and delivery was electrifying. I did indeed feel that I was the man he was talking about, that I was a sinner without hope and that without Christ I would be eternally lost. He ended his sermon by asking us to close our eyes in prayer and to repeat silently the words he was about to speak if we wanted to know Christ personally. I did and that night I knew that Christ had come into my life. It was also special for me in terms of my future. As I bowed my head and repeated those words I had this strong impression that I too would do the work that David Shepherd was doing. That my role in life was to explain the Bible to people and bring them hope. This was more than a passing idea; it came to me as a kind of invitation from God, a "call" if you like. That evening was God's invitation to become a shepherd of his flock and a minister of his grace to others.

Maybe not seismic, possibly unintelligible to those not interested in religious matters, but this was important to my father. He had now embraced two different Christian narratives. Both had crisis built into them but of a different order. That evening in Gorseinon,

Dad opened his heart and mind to evangelical Christianity where the crisis was of a personal nature. Faith in God came by way of a conversion, an inner upheaval, where the broad way of destruction was jettisoned for the narrow way of eternal life. Its claims were exclusive, and tolerance of other ways and religions was limited. The other expression of Christian faith he had embraced was rather different. Following Jesus meant going into the world to share his love and build the kingdom of God. It was a way which spoke about the wideness of God's mercy, and a kingdom demonstrated in social justice, campaigning for the rights of the poor, lifting people out of poverty and oppression, and resisting warfare. And God's kingdom wasn't the property of the church but God's and he could use anyone whose imagination had been fuelled by the example of Jesus. This was how Muriel Lester formed such deep relationships with Gandhi and Rabindrath Tagore, and how she collaborated with people of all faiths and none within the International Fellowship of Reconciliation. This approach also allowed Toyohiko Kagawa to dream of a million souls won for Christ, by which he meant better housing and welfare as much as eternal life.

Dad felt inspired and provoked by that evening's events in Gorseinon:

I felt excited by everything. Christianity was no longer a sideline, something I did on a Sunday. I somehow felt as though Christ was now central to everything in the world. And even though there were these dreadful stories about the escalation of tension in Europe and the rest of the world, I couldn't help but feel a kind of joy within. After that evening listening to David Shepherd, I had a conviction about faith I'd never known before. But the summer schools and the books I was reading had opened up to me the vast opportunities ahead of the church. And I could be part of it! Who knows, maybe I too could travel and see what was happening in the world?

CHAPTER 8

1936 and the Rise of Nationalism

The *Bibl Sanctaidd* (Holy Bible), published circa 1863 by E. Slater, publisher, bookseller, and bookbinder, 24 Chapel Street, Bradford, is a large hardcover family Bible, complete with lead borders, once affixed by two locks, now missing. It is entirely in Welsh and contains chapter notes written by the Reverend Peter Williams and illustrations and prints after Poussin, Carracci, and Rubens. Between the Old and New Testaments are pages dedicated to capturing family births, marriages, and deaths. Only one branch of the family is recorded – that of my father's maternal grandfather John Russel (as spelled on the page). He was born in Dowlais, near Merthyr, in 1840. John's father William was probably Scottish, and worked in the steel works in Abertillery before moving to Merthyr Tydfil with his wife Hannah. John's wife, Catherine Davies, was born in 1845 in Allt Wen, a small hamlet in the Swansea Valley near Pontardawe. John and Catherine had five children, and after Catherine's untimely death, John moved to the Gower and married again. His new wife, Elizabeth Richards, came from a family of farmers. Together they had a further four children: William, Delia, Minnie, and my grandmother Martha.

This Bible made a sudden appearance in my parents' home in about 2009. It was apparently a gift from a distant cousin of my father who lived on the Gower and wanted him to have it. It was the truncated family tree in its middle pages that gave my dad an uncomfortable revelation: his grandfather on his mother's side was not Scottish. From an early age, he had been told that John Russel was born in the Highlands of Scotland and tracked his way to the Welsh valleys as the Industrial Revolution opened up new opportunities.

My mother regaled us with tales of her father's Scottish heritage, although when I was given the Bible I realised that her father was actually Welsh. The Scottish, Russell, connection must have come through John Russell's father. But it is a puzzle, since my mother was able to speak words in Gaelic and also count to ten in the Northumbrian dialect, which she said her father had learnt after working in the mines in Northumberland.

This Bible had a linguistic importance in our family. On both sides of my father's family, paternal and maternal, Welsh had been the dominant language for generations. And many homes in nineteenth-century Wales would have displayed two books on the mantelpiece. One would have been a copy of the Welsh Bible, translated by Bishop William Morgan in 1588, and the other a Welsh translation of *The Pilgrim's Progress*, *Taith y Pererin*, translated by Thomas Jones in 1699 – an extremely successful and enterprising almanac maker, bookseller, printer, and publisher.

The impact of Bishop Morgan's Welsh Bible was incalculable. It was published in 1588, a few years ahead of the English version authorized by King James in 1611. Morgan translated the Scriptures from original Hebrew and Greek texts and also drew heavily on an earlier Welsh version of the New Testament produced by William Salesbury in 1567. After his labours, William Morgan was made Bishop of Llandaf and later became Bishop of St Asaph. Not only did his translation bring the Bible alive to non-Latin readers in Wales for the first time, it also promoted literacy and education for the masses. Like Luther and Tyndale before him, he discovered that Bible translation had a transformative effect on culture, way beyond the religious significance of the text.

> *Both my parents spoke Welsh, although curiously they spoke English to each other and Welsh with their children.*

And this phenomenon was true also of my childhood. Both my parents spoke Welsh to us as children but used English between themselves. Until their deaths, it always felt unnatural addressing them in English. Patriotic, fervent champions of Welsh culture, my father flirted with Welsh nationalist aspirations during his late teenage years but found them incompatible with his internationalist Christian convictions.

> *I was intoxicated by the history of the church and the huge optimism for world mission. I'd never travelled beyond my patch of Wales and yet I was devouring literature that shrank the globe and made me aware of other cultures and languages. Even prayer meetings, which had once seemed the deadliest of all gatherings, built bridges into other nations. Nationalism seemed tame, idolatrous even, compared to the scope of the gospel.*

Nevertheless in 1936 he came close to pursuing the cause of Welsh nationalism, provoked by an incident that inspired his pacifist beliefs.

In 1936 the War Office made a compulsory seizure order on an old farm complex, Penyberth, on the Llyn Peninsula in the north-west of Wales. Despite considerable local opposition, and there being two other proposed English sites (Abbotsbury and Northumberland), an RAF school of bombing was built there, reflecting the growing official anxiety over Germany's arms stockpiling.

Penyberth was in an almost entirely Welsh-speaking part of the country, and this intervention was seen as an act of gross insensitivity on the part of the government. Anxieties were expressed about the school's negative impact on local culture, both linguistically and because of the imperial militarism it would inevitably champion. But Stanley Baldwin, the prime minister, was adamant that the historic farmhouse be demolished and the school constructed.

It was an area where the Welsh-speaking chapels were at their strongest and I would imagine that the vast majority of people were pacifist in their leanings. You can't begin to imagine how disillusioned people felt after the First World War. It was meant to be a war to end all wars and usher in a better deal for smaller nations. The big bullies of the world were to be tamed and democracy given its rightful place. But all we could see was Germany flexing its muscles and Britain yet again preparing to fight another wasted war.

Three men led the charge against Baldwin's government and they all held strong Christian convictions: Saunders Lewis, a Catholic university lecturer, writer, and playwright who was prominent in the National Party of Wales, Plaid Genedlaethol Cymru (later Plaid Cymru); D. J. Williams, a Baptist schoolmaster in Fishguard, Pembrokeshire; and Lewis Valentine, a Baptist minister and one of the most celebrated preachers of his day. Having served in the First World War, he had written extensively about his experiences and was an avowed pacifist. He had stood unsuccessfully for Parliament as a Welsh nationalist in 1929 and was at this time serving a church in Llandudno:

> I'd heard Lewis Valentine preach in local meetings and he
> was a fine speaker. Like the other men I admired, he was
> a man of prayer, of learning and action. He seemed totally
> fearless and saw no contradiction with being a Christian,
> nationalist and pacifist.

One night in November 1936, and after prolonged discussion amongst themselves and others, the three men set fire to the sheds and offices on the RAF building site at Penyberth. So remote and unpopulated was the immediate vicinity that the three men retired to a motor car and discussed poetry and philosophy before driving to Pwllheli police station and handing themselves in.

The original trial in Caernarfon was inconclusive, with the jury unable to reach a verdict. Popular opinion was enraged by the decision to move the retrial to the Old Bailey and at Swansea University's decision to remove Saunders Lewis from his post before the trial finished. Further national disquiet occurred when the judge repeatedly made scathing remarks about Welsh culture, language, and nationalism.

The Old Bailey trial was reported widely at the time and I felt immensely proud of the three men, particularly Lewis Valentine, with whom I felt I had a great deal in common. I remember reading that he saw this action as part of a protest against warfare and that no one had been hurt in the attack. I was particularly moved when he said that on the morning of the bombing he had taken his daughter to school for the first time. He knew that he would go to prison for his actions but he didn't want her to grow up in a Europe congested with bombs and missiles. Something had to be done, he said, and he was willing to pay the price. Despite interruptions from the judge and the prosecuting counsel, he said that the people of Wales and Britain didn't want another war and to be part of a system of stock-piling weapons. He felt they had no choice in what they had done. The way to deal with an enemy was not by imitating their means as a kind of tit for tat but through dialogue, diplomacy and reason. The more England stock-piled arms, the more other countries would do the same until there would be bombing everywhere.

He was saying the things I believed in. That you couldn't remain silent in the face of wrong doing, even if it was the government you were opposing. I too believed there was a higher law to which I was accountable, to which my conscience was accountable. I even remember reading that at one point Lewis Valentine said, "Better death than shame."

It was the insistence on conscience that stayed with me. Here were three good men prepared to commit an illegal action on the basis that doing nothing would be complicit in an even worse offence against morality and God. That's what I admired about them. Not the nationalism or the statements that Wales was being press ganged into England's war, but their ferocious commitment to doing the right thing whatever the cost. And the fact also that these three men did what they did as a Christian act. It made them offensive to the judge and to the press but my estimation of them couldn't be higher. They went on record to say that their allegiance to Christ and his cause was greater than any loyalty to the law of England. My problem with it all was that the Kingdom of God and Welsh nationalism seemed to be interchangeable, and that disturbed me profoundly. I instinctively felt that nationalism and fascism were not strangers and I wanted no part in either.

It was a strange period because after both trials, I recall that Lewis Valentine was greatly in demand as a preacher. I'm sure he came to the Swansea area at least once if not more in a matter of months and that's when I went to hear him. He took as his text a verse in chapter five of the Acts of the Apostles. "We must obey God rather than men." He brilliantly expounded the verse from the early church's clash with the authorities to modern day Wales. He had us eating out of the palm of his hand. He was an electrifying preacher; biblical, learned, humorous at times, passionate but very sincere. He was no empty pulpiteer, performing for his fans. And at the end of the sermon, I witnessed something I had never seen before or after. The congregation applauded the preacher, as though to say we're behind you, your cause is our cause. This however did make me feel uneasy: that a man was being applauded instead of Christ. And looking at his reaction, he too looked awkward and embarrassed. But nevertheless there was a tremendous sense of solidarity and unity around him.

An English jury found all three men guilty of the charges laid against them. On 19 January 1937, they were sentenced to nine months' imprisonment in Wormwood Scrubs prison. During their imprisonment, the German Luftwaffe bombed the Republican town of Guernica, Spain, on 26 April 1937. This bombing resulted in 1,654 civilian fatalities, largely women and children, and at the time it was the worst recorded incident of aerial bombardment. Many in Wales saw this as a chilling fulfilment of Valentine's words that the arms race would simply lead to greater and more indiscriminate bombings.

None of this however was enough to sway my father. Far from becoming a Welsh nationalist, he refused to identify himself with its causes or programmes. Even though Plaid Cymru contained many pacifists with similar backgrounds, he took exception to the party's ambivalent attitude towards Nazism. In 1939 its president, J. E. Daniels, described the looming conflict as a clash of two imperial powers that would not benefit Wales. There is even some evidence of a planned Plaid Cymru delegation to Germany to make some sort of a deal with Hitler. One academic has even suggested that Gwynfor Evans (later MP for Carmarthen) considered that a German victory might enhance Wales' independent aspirations. In his small book, *Heddychiaeth Gristnogol yng Nghymru* (Christian Pacifism in Wales), Gwynfor Evans stated that many Welsh nationalists who were also pacifists saw the looming conflict as England's war; one that Wales would be wise to avoid. Evans suggested that a number of nationalists hoped that through making concessions to the Germans it might be possible to secretly support the anti-Nazi activists trying to get rid of Hitler. Evans quotes a prominent Welsh nationalist pacifist at the time, Dewi Prys Thomas:

I am a Welsh Christian, and as a citizen of Wales I believe in my nation's right to freedom, like every other nation. A Czech man would refuse to fight for the German army as would a Finnish man for the Russians. I am Welsh and I oppose any attempts to make me fight for England's army.[1]

The ease with which the nationalists were willing to hang their colours on the most convenient peg seemed to John to lack principle and was driven by a pragmatism he viewed as selfish, if not dangerous. Decades later, when he was a minister of Capel Seion in his beloved Llanelli, he felt uneasy at the impact of Welsh nationalism on Christianity:

What is absolutely fundamental is that the church communicates the message of Christ and makes disciples. This is the heart of the matter, and culture, language and nationalism are in danger of becoming idols that distract us from our true love.

Dad was awkward when having to identify with any particular stream or group. He saw himself, essentially, as an outsider, someone who didn't quite belong. This was a perpetual theme in his life, which to me explains how torn he felt about many matters.

As Dad continued as a sales assistant with Morris the Realm, the country went through a constitutional crisis with the abdication of Edward VIII, who wanted to marry an American divorcee, Wallis Simpson. After a turbulent period as prime minister, lurching from disarmament to rearmament, Stanley Baldwin retired. He had remained at the helm during the crisis, but now passed the baton to Neville Chamberlain. Chamberlain sought to bring in populist domestic policies, and his Factories

Act created better working conditions for women and children and prescribed the maximum hours that could be worked each day. His foreign policy, in terms of the relationship with Germany, was one of appeasement. Having witnessed the horrors and waste of the First World War, and lost close family members, he and his new cabinet hoped that diplomacy would triumph and that a new deal in Europe could be brokered. This was the consensus of the cabinet and indeed Parliament, although there were dissenting voices, including that of Winston Churchill.

The influence of the Germany–Italy–Japan axis was growing. Japan had launched an attack on China, threatening a number of key British empire installations. Hitler was forging links with a new far right party that had emerged in Austria, prompting disquiet over the German Chancellor's ambitions in that country. The Spanish Civil War was reaching a desperate tipping point as General Franco's government was now recognized by Germany, Italy, and the Vatican in November 1936. With bitter internal disputes dividing the Republican camp, the balance of power now lay with Franco, who had greater international support and a far deeper supply of resources.

My father's sight however was less on international issues, and more on his own immediate aspirations to become an ordained church minister:

> By Easter 1937, I was convinced that I wanted to become a minister of the gospel. Not only was this a strong personal conviction but one that had been confirmed by my minister, friends and the church members at Noddfa. When the day came for my "trial sermon" in Noddfa, the most dreadful thing happened. On the basis of my delivery and content that day, I would either succeed or fail in candidating for

ministerial training. Just before the evening service was to start, our minister suffered a catastrophic heart attack and was rushed to hospital unconscious. The meeting went ahead and I preached, but he was dead within the hour, leaving a widow and family. It was a terribly sad period for everyone.

One major obstacle however lay ahead of me. Since I hadn't matriculated from school, I was denied access to higher education, a prerequisite for ministerial training. In those days every minister had to be of university standard, which meant of course achieving a satisfactory pass in the Matric. After seemingly endless interviews and assessments, the local Baptist association recommended me for training on condition that I spent a year at a preparatory college in Trefeca, high up in the Black Mountains. During that year I would study for and pass the Matric and also learn the rudiments of New Testament Greek and Hebrew. Latin was already a compulsory subject within the Matric. Curiously enough, because of my proficiency in Latin, I was allowed to take this instead of Mathematics, which was a great relief. For some reason or another I was hopeless at Maths, even though my work at Morris the Realm required me to be quick at mental calculation.

The family were delighted by the news, and I think proud that someone from the family was able to go to university. Mam and Dat told me separately that I was the first of any generation to go to college and I should seize the opportunities afforded to me. They were also pleased that I was going into the ministry and wouldn't have to endure the brutality of life in the tin works or underground. But I confess I had mixed feelings. My income had made a world of difference to the family's financial fortunes and my studies

*would now have a detrimental effect on them. And even
though my two older sisters, Madge and Nancy, were now
married, Ceinwen was still at home. So in reality I was
in two minds about it all. In fact, the reality was I would
probably need some financial support from my parents from
time to time. There was no student grant and somehow I
would need to support myself. I found out however that I
would be required to conduct church services every Sunday
around South Wales, and I would no doubt receive enough to
live on. The college in Trefeca was remote but I was told that
preaching opportunities would be plentiful; enough to see me
through each week.*

*The family were amazing. My sister Madge and her
husband Vincent supported my parents financially, making
up the deficit of the income I was no longer bringing into
the home. But they went the extra mile and also promised
to subsidise my living expenses whilst in college. And even
though they were as poor as chapel mice, Mam and Dat
said they had saved a bit of money for my education. It was
round about then that Mam started referring to another well
known Russell who might help. She said "John, our relation
Lord John Russell was prime minister of Britain in the last
century and I have it in good authority that there's money
waiting for us in Chancery."*

We are still waiting.

CHAPTER 9

1938, a Year of Preparation

I am holding *Macaulay's Miscellaneous Writings and Speeches*, published by Longmans, Green and Co of 39 Paternoster Row, London, in 1900. Bound in hardcover, this dark green volume showcases the literary and political writing of Thomas Babington Macaulay, 1st Baron Macaulay (1800–59). Celebrated both as an essayist and a Parliamentarian, Macaulay was a prolific writer and Whig politician. In cabinet he served as Secretary at War and Paymaster General, but it is as a writer that he is best remembered. His style was direct, straightforward, and opinionated – addressed more to the masses than to the establishment.

This was one of my father's textbooks during his preparatory year before a further period of formal college training to become a Baptist minister. The curriculum for the year was broad, preparing students for the all-important Matriculation exam as well as elementary tuition in Hebrew and New Testament Greek. Several other books from that period have survived but this one is significant to me. To begin with, it reminds me that dad was widely read, particularly enjoying history and the biographies of eminent people. A good story well told gave him pleasure and it mattered not to him whether the subject of the biography shared his religious or political views. But this volume is important for another reason. An inscription on the inside cover page identifies its owner: D. Jones, Trevecca College, 23.03.05. Of the owner, I know nothing, but the address given played an important part in my father's history. In English it is known as Trevecca College and in Welsh it is *Coleg Trefeca*.

Set in the Black Mountains, near Talgarth, the college was originally founded as a religious community by the revivalist Howell Harris in 1752. Closely associated with John Wesley and George Whitefield, Harris was a tireless preacher around Wales and his efforts led to the foundation of the Calvinistic Methodists, who later became the Presbyterian Church of Wales. Harris called his community *Teulu Trefeca* (the Trefeca family) and on the ceiling of the large parlour a great painted eye is still visible, reminding all within that God is all-seeing and all-knowing.

After his death, Trefeca was closely associated with the Countess of Huntingdon Connexion, a church movement founded by Selina, Countess of Huntingdon, in 1738. In the eighteenth century it was yet again associated with another religious revival, this time centred on Revd Thomas Charles, who founded the Bible Society. Following denominational changes in the early twentieth century, the college's academic faculty moved to Aberystwyth, and Trefeca reopened in 1905 as a preparatory college for men seeking university ministerial training from the Baptist and Congregational denominations. Even though it was a college, the title of headmaster was preferred to that of principal. The building was a mix of Georgian architecture with later influences. Lectures and seminars took place in the main house, with dormitory accommodation in other blocks behind the main building.

John's bus ride from Swansea to the college in September 1938 was his greatest journey to date. Most of his life had been spent shuttling around the Swansea area, with occasional forays east to the industrial valleys. But this adventure took him into the mountains of Brecknockshire. Much of the sixty-mile trip led him through the Swansea Valley, the lower reaches of which were cloaked in the steam and smog of mines and steel works. He passed Ystalyfera and thought about his grandparents. By the time they arrived in Ystradgynlais, the stained rim of heavy industry had been left behind; now there were only green meadows, hills, and waterfalls. Accompanying him on the bus were a number of men whom he had met before:

For the previous few summers, I had been attending a range of courses hosted by the Baptist denomination in Ilston. It was there I heard Muriel Lester speak on the Kingdom of God and the need for radical discipleship. The culture that gave me spiritual nurture was expansive and generous, and even though we were all Welsh speakers, there was a real sense of being part of the world church. Many of my friends at that time became missionaries in India and Brazil. Most of the men I'd met on those summer courses were also in Trefeca and indeed our friendship was lifelong.

As he made his way along the gravel path to the college's imposing entrance and entered the main house, his senses were bombarded with new stimuli. New colleagues greeted him. Strong aromas wafted by, of polished floors and cooked food coming from the kitchen. John was part of a cohort of twenty-two male students, all preparing for church ministry within the Baptist denomination. Like Dad, they had all passed their elementary exams, but for one reason or another they had not matriculated. Without any national system of benefits for sickness or unemployment, most of these young men had been forced to leave school at the age of fifteen in order to support their families. Students were given tuition in English, Welsh, Mathematics, Latin, History, and Geography in addition to the rudiments of New Testament Greek and biblical Hebrew.

John would have noticed the various paintings and photographs of former alumni which hung on the walls. Before that term was completed his year was also caught on film. The sepia and grainy academic class photo for 1938 features a group of suited and earnest young men flanking the three gowned academic staff; some looked like boy preachers about to launch into pulpit rhetoric. A few of the students were in their late twenties, but the vast majority were several years younger. With groomed hair, seven pairs of (round) spectacles, and no facial hair to be seen, they were all ready to serve their denomination. Thirteen of them signed the back of John's photograph, along with the names of their home towns and churches.

Some didn't, including Gerald Griffiths: tall, blond, with a telling handkerchief peeping over his breast pocket. A man with film star looks, he would cross the Atlantic and pastor a large church in Toronto. My dad counted two others among his closest friends and I remember their visits to us. Oswald Tregelles Williams, from Soar Morriston, seems younger than the others with his boyish complexion, porcine cheeks, and sardonic smile. His angled posture suggests a rakish self-confidence; he would later become the BBC's Head of Religious Affairs. And in his retirement he mentored me in my attempts at becoming a radio broadcaster on Swansea Sound. The studious-looking Elvet Cox, from Pen y Bank, Ammanford, would be one of my father's best men at his wedding. And then there was my father, whose demeanour and position spoke volumes about him. At the back, standing a little behind Gerald Griffiths, his head leans gently towards the right. Not exactly in the shadows but the whole occasion was probably making him feel awkward. Even though he was among friends, he didn't quite fit.

Another who did not sign the photo was Harry Bowen, also from Llanelli, whose face looked as if it was about to burst into uncontrollable gurning. Dad developed a close bond with him. Most of the students came from financially strapped homes but Harry's background was even more disadvantaged. Combined with several impediments, he had had to fight his way to Trefeca:

Harry didn't think he was going to do very well that year. He seemed very bright to me and his knowledge of the Bible was encyclopaedic. He had the most mischievous sense of humour of anyone I'd met before and he was a fund of endless anecdotes and stories. I remember him telling me once of a bell-ringing episode when he was a boy. His chapel was hosting some special services and a well known preacher had been invited. Harry was so exercised by the apparent apathy of the people on his street he marched out at six o'clock in the morning with a hand bell shouting "Codwch chi diawlaid, dyma dydd yr Arglwydd!" (Wake up you devils, it's the Lord's Day!)

But poor Harry had a kind of nervous tick which meant that his face was constantly in a spasm. This feature had no bearing on his powers of speech and he was the most delightful of friends. I found him totally fascinating but this strange syndrome, whatever it was, resulted in no self-confidence as far as academic work was concerned.

And Harry's concerns were well-founded; later, John wrote:

[Harry] was naturally brighter than most of the men in Trefeca but he barely had any secondary education. I don't think he'd even passed his elementary exams. He'd known crippling poverty at home, largely due to unemployment. His father had been severely injured in an industrial accident when Harry was a boy and he became the main breadwinner to keep a roof over their heads. He was so far behind the rest of us that he never matriculated and so was unable to go to university. He trained at the Baptist college in Cardiff and was a minister all his working life but it grieved him deeply that he missed out on a degree. The older he got, the greater the sense of injustice and bitterness he felt at his misfortune.

I remember Harry visiting my dad when I was a teenager and we lived in Cardiff. I too was transfixed by his liquid, changing features. He sounded like Huw Griffith, a pompously funny Welsh actor made famous by Ealing Studios and David Lean. He looked like the risqué comedian Frankie Howerd, his face alive with uncontrollable and suggestive twitching. Unlike Howerd, his mannerisms were entirely innocent and involuntary. Even the purpose of his visit to us was eccentric; in nearby Albany Road was an umbrella hospital to which he had taken his sick appliance. Whilst awaiting surgery, he called in on my parents.

Harry died at the beginning of 1993 and my father attended his funeral, as noted in his diary of that year:

I arrived a little late for the beginning of the service at Caersalem and was a little disappointed that it was being held not in the chapel but in the vestry. Since that was crowded I had to stand, along with others, around the door, and whilst I was able to hear, I could not see any of those who took part... My heart was full as I thought of bygone days, the goodness of God in giving me the friendship of HB and Elvet Cox while at Ilston and subsequently in college and in the ministry.

With students who were drawn exclusively from South Wales, particularly the area of heavy industry, the intellectual climate in Trefeca was a heady mix of piety, theological inquiry, and radical politics. My dad's inquiring mind and appetite for spirituality were being stimulated around the clock. No longer at the beck and call of customers or family, he delved into the world of books and debate. For the first time he encountered the new scholarship from Germany that challenged the traditional understanding of the Bible and its teaching. Known as Higher Criticism, this new discipline exposed the Bible to the rigours of linguistics, archaeology, and anthropology, and tore it to shreds. The Old Testament, it said, was the product of competing literary sources and the book of Genesis in particular could not be taken literally in the light of evolutionary science. The New Testament was also placed under the microscope of scholarship and found to be wanting. Miracles, angels, the virgin birth, resurrection, even the divinity of Christ were deemed to be inventions of later church communities inserted back into the text. This was generally referred to as a liberal view of the Bible and became the dominant theological approach taught in universities in continental Europe and the UK, especially during the late nineteenth century and the first few decades of the twentieth.

But not all John's teaching went that way, and during his lectures, he was introduced to the work of the brilliant Swiss theologian Karl Barth, whose commentary on Romans appeared in English in 1933. Such was this work's devastating critique of liberal theology, it led one scholar, Karl Adam, to remark, "It fell like a bombshell on the theologians' playground."

Without apology, Barth swam against the tide of fashionable scholarly opinion, arguing that God could only be known through the crucified Christ. Any attempt to twin God with human culture, government, achievements, possessions, even nature itself, was simply idolatry. Scripture revealed God's thoughts about humanity, and not humanity's attempt to understand the divine. In this commentary and subsequent works, Barth was highly critical of liberal theology, not least because he had witnessed many of his much-lauded and influential teachers signing up to the Kaiser's war aims.

Such was the impact of this commentary, Barth was headhunted by several prestigious German universities. But yet again he witnessed the same capitulation to totalitarian power on the part of the churches, and along with a number of other theologians and pastors he joined a kind of resistance movement, the German Confessing Church, which was opposed to the Nazification of German Protestantism.

Soon after his appointment as Chancellor in 1933, Hitler formulated a plan for a Reich Church (*Reichskirche*), which would reorganize the twenty-seven Protestant regional churches in Germany into a single, national church under the leadership of a national bishop. On 28 June 1933, Ludwig Müller, a prominent Nazi, became Reich Bishop (*Reichsbischof*), and the Nazi "Führer Principle" was adopted. This meant that the church, along with other civic bodies and private citizens, recognized Hitler's ultimate jurisdiction over them. Some prominent members of this new church advocated a complete abandonment of the Old Testament, because of its Jewish heritage, and sought to introduce the so-called Aryan paragraph into their constitution. This allowed organizations to limit membership to Aryans only.

In response to this initiative, a Lutheran pastor, Martin Niemöller, sent a letter to all German pastors, inviting them to join a Pastors' Emergency League. In 1934 this league created the German Confessing Church in opposition to Müller's appointment and policies. The Confessing Church took its name from the fact that its members had pledged themselves to affirm the great historic confessions of the church. In Barmen, on 29–31 May 1934, its leaders met to articulate their values and beliefs. The subsequent Barmen Declaration, drafted largely by Karl Barth, was unequivocal in its opposition to all attempts to redefine Christianity. The preamble contained a warning that commonly held Christian beliefs and values were now being seriously undermined by these new developments:

> It is threatened by the teaching methods and actions of the ruling Church party of the "German Christians" and of the Church administration carried on by them.[1]

This opening declaration stated forcibly that "alien principles" had now invaded the German church and unless these were challenged, this church was in danger of falling apart. The Barmen Declaration went on to define six confessions which reminded Christians of their exclusive allegiance to Jesus Christ. These truths took the form of six clauses based on Bible verses which emphasized Jesus' unique authority over the individual, the church, and the world. Each verse was then followed by a short interpretative statement and after that the repeating phrase "we reject the false doctrine", which was itself followed by some principle that Müller wanted to foist on them.

For instance, the fifth clause of the Barmen Declaration began with a quotation from 1 Peter 2:17: "Fear God, honour the emperor" [NIV]. This was then followed by a short interpretation, affirming that the state was divinely ordained to provide justice and peace and to protect its citizens through force if necessary. The fifth clause then ends like this:

> We reject the false doctrine, as though the State, over and beyond its special commission, should and could become the single and totalitarian order of human life, thus fulfilling the Church's vocation as well.[2]

Within two years of the Barmen Declaration, hundreds of pastors in the German Confessing Church had been arrested, their assets confiscated by the state, and church offerings banned. These included pastors such as Martin Niemöller and Hermann Ludwig Maas who also helped evacuate Jews from Germany.

John's exposure to the Barmen Declaration caused him to reflect on his own views as war loomed:

The situation in Britain was utterly different to Germany's. They were the aggressor trying to provoke hostility and conflict, but the Barmen Declaration had a relevance to us too. Whilst accepting that governmental authority was ordained by God, they were not higher than him and had no right to impose its will upon the conscience of a believer. I had to obey my conscience and that conscience had to be submissive to God's Word. This meant that if our government demanded that I fight and kill another, then I must resist. "Thou shalt not kill" was an imperative command to all believers at all times.

*I think Barth's assault on liberal theology also made
me think again about some of my influences. Much of the
Kingdom of God movement was based on wishful thinking,
without recognising the destructive power of human sin.
What was required was the transformation of society
through transformed people and this was only possible
through the cross of Christ.*

The worsening international situation was not lost on these young students in Trefeca. Before they had arrived at their preparatory college in 1938, the government passed the Emergency Powers (Defence) Act, enabling it to take certain measures in defence of the nation and to maintain public order. In all, the Act contained around 100 measures, ranging from calling up military reservists, to appointing Air Raid Precaution volunteers and creating several other voluntary organizations needed during wartime.

*From the beginning of my time in Trefeca, much of the
conversation between the students inevitably focused on
events in Germany and the choices facing Britain. We all had
an interest in current affairs and at times these exchanges
could become heated. It would be fair to say that most of
us took an appeasement line, although a smaller number
felt that the German threat was so great that the situation
required a more decisive military approach. Views were
also polarised among the staff too I think. The college had
something of a record with regard to the First World War.
Four students had lost their lives during that conflict and this
was the cause of some pride on the part of the headmaster in
particular, although other teachers took a dissenting line.*

By spring 1939, further legislation was passed requiring all men aged between twenty and twenty-two to sign up for military duty. The Military Training Act of 27 April 1939 commanded all fit and able men to register for six months of military training followed by placement on a reserve list in the event of war.

We were about to start our Matriculation exams and this new law was deeply unsettling. We'd spent months learning and cramming and suddenly we were now under the scrutiny of the government. Most of us took the view that as full time students training for the ministry we should carry on as normal and keep working for the Matric. We were so close to the prospect of going to university and Baptist college, we couldn't just stumble at the last fence. Our teachers told us that there would be time to register after exams and we should carry on as normal and worry about this new law in a few weeks' time. They felt sure that our accrediting denominations would be able to advise us then.

But it was not scholarship that was exercising the German mind: Hitler had designs on restoring the nation's lost pride. After the end of the First World War, the Treaty of Versailles imposed what the Germans viewed as severe restrictions on German military and foreign policy. Unification with Austria (*Anschluss*) was forbidden, as was any German military presence in the Rhineland to the east of France. Germany's borders in the east were clipped by the creation of the Polish corridor, which linked that country to the city of Danzig on the coast, and cut the German province of East Prussia off from the rest of Germany. Hitler dreamed of a larger, more powerful fatherland, and believed that the German master race had the right to take lands held by those races he viewed as subhuman – which included the Slavs of eastern Europe. By 1938, he had remilitarized the German Rhineland, built up the German armed forces, and annexed Austria. But none of the other European powers, including Great Britain, passed comment, partly because they were also concerned by the threat of Stalinist Russia, and viewed Germany as an important buffer state.

Hitler's ambitions continued as he looked across to Sudetenland, the German-speaking area of Czechoslovakia. This nation had also been formed in the aftermath of World War One and Hitler wanted to reclaim Sudetenland as part of Germany. Thus on 29 September 1938, he met with UK prime minister Neville Chamberlain and French prime minister Édouard Daladier in Munich and they accepted his proposal provided he did not invade other countries. They hoped that by conceding some territory to the Germans, another world war could be avoided. Despite Czech opposition, the Munich agreement was signed by major European powers in September 1938 and the annexation of Sudetenland recognized. But Hitler's hunger for further German expansion was not satisfied. Having invaded the rest of Czechoslovakia, he demanded access to the Danzig corridor, Polish territory. Alarmed, the British government in turn guaranteed Polish sovereignty, and promised to intervene if necessary. After a year of fruitless negotiations, and having signed a friendship pact with Stalin, Hitler gave Poland a final ultimatum late in August 1939 and threatened invasion on 1 September unless his demands were met. No doubt he thought that, once again, Chamberlain would complain – but not take any action.

John successfully completed his year at Trefeca and matriculated in the summer of 1939. Accepted both by the South Wales Baptist College and by Cardiff University, he would soon make a decision that would define the rest of his life.

CHAPTER 10

Sunday 1 September 1939

I am looking at a large framed commemorative certificate with photographs and illustrations. It announces that it was "presented by the British Steel Smelters Amalgamated Association to Brother Thomas Jones by the officers and members of the Grovesend Branch, February 10 1916, in appreciation of valued services rendered as President during 1915" and is signed by:

Henry Davies, President

H. Thomas, Vice President

E. John, Treasurer

D. Rasbridge, Secretary.

My grandfather, Dat, was one of the founder members of the Grovesend Branch of the British Steel Smelters Amalgamated Association. He started in the tin works at the age of fourteen in 1894 and was made President of this union in 1915, aged thirty-five. On 1 January 1917, this union merged with the Mill, Iron and Tinplate Workers, the Associated Iron and Steel Workers of Great Britain, and the National Steel Workers' Association Engineering and Labour League to form the Iron and Steel Trader Confederation (ISTC). On 1 July 2004, the ISTC merged with several other unions to form the Community union. The framed certificate now has pride of place in a cousin's home in Cardiff.

In addition to a photograph portraying working life in the rolling mill where Dat worked, there is also a head and shoulders photograph of him. There are also numerous coloured illustrations showing both the contribution of steel and tin to British industry and also the benefits of belonging to the union.

It's the date that's important. This was presented to Dat less than a month before the Military Services Act came into force and it recognized his presidency in 1915. As soon as conscription was enforced, as we have seen, this father of two attempted to sign up for military service. He was informed that he would not be accepted, because he was in a reserved occupation. Instead, he was sent to work in a munitions factory in Southampton.

Twenty-three years later and his only son was facing a similar decision. The National Service (Armed Forces) Act had been passed with immediate effect, replacing the earlier Military Training Act. John had to make a choice. His would be totally different.

On 1 September 1939, Germany invaded Poland and John was conducting a Sunday service:

I was preaching at a small church in Carmarthenshire. We were all expecting an announcement from the government about the crisis with Germany, so about ten minutes before 11 o'clock the church secretary stood up, and gave a rather awkward notice "Due to the grave events unfolding in London and Germany, the service will end a little earlier." He thanked me for preaching a shorter sermon and seemed then to apologise to God! The poor man was clearly unsettled by the change to the normal order but blustered and flustered his way through the announcements. With that we retired to a hall at the back of the church where there was a large wireless. Everyone was orderly; we sat in rows of chairs and waited anxiously for 11 o'clock. The congregation was apparently considerably larger that day as a number of people without wirelesses at home had come to hear the prime minister and not the preacher!

This disturbed sabbath day was replicated across Britain as all ages huddled around wireless sets and listened to Prime Minister Neville Chamberlain's chilling admission that his diplomacy had failed. These are the words my father heard:

This morning the British Ambassador in Berlin handed the German government a final note stating that unless we heard from them by 11 o'clock that they were prepared at once to withdraw their troops from Poland, a state of war would exist between us.

I have to tell you now that no such undertaking has been received, and that consequently this country is at war with Germany.

The mood in the crowded hall was subdued:

There was a profound sense of shock, even though everyone knew it was coming. I'd hoped that reason would prevail and a talking solution might be possible. Chamberlain and Baldwin before him were not war mongers and I believed they had done their best but to no avail. As we walked

*silently out of the church and into the fine autumn day we
all knew that life was going to change for the worse. It was
a peculiar feeling; we were now at war and yet everything
was normal. Sundays were always quiet anyway, but the
birds were singing, sun shining and all seemed well with the
world. Except of course that everything would now be geared
towards warfare.*

*The train journey back to Gorseinon was very quiet.
Everyone was quiet, caught in their own reverie, wondering
what the future now held for us all. One thought dominated
me as I stared blankly out of the carriage window: what
would I do next? We had been living with this possibility for
years now and I had debated the matter passionately, voicing
my pacifist convictions. But that day, like everyone else, the
reality of the situation was dawning on me. The theory of
war was over and the fighting would soon begin. All that
futile diplomacy! As I listened to Neville Chamberlain's
announcement on the Home Service my heart sank. The
last war was meant to end all others but here we were again
facing an escalating conflict. I was so disappointed that
the argument for appeasement had failed. It all seemed so
hopeful a few months ago; a rational and Christian way of
defusing the crisis on the Continent. But today marked the
end of all that hope; where was this going to take us? I could
not and would not fight. Everything within me said it was
wrong, unthinkable, to take another's life.*

Despite the apparent normality of everything, the mood was tense.
More Anderson shelters started appearing in people's gardens,
in case of air raids, and from time to time, a loud wailing sound
would eclipse all else:

*There were regular public information broadcasts by the
government, telling the population what to do and what to
avoid. We were told that at the threat of aerial attack, air
raid sirens would sound and we were to immediately seek
shelter. We were told that these sirens would sound twice a
day for the next few weeks so that we became accustomed
to them and could locate the nearest shelters. People could
purchase their own shelters, or local authorities would make
large ones available if you were near them or you could
simply hide under a table in the safest part of your house. It
was all very disturbing. From the very beginning, a horrid
anxiety was introduced into people's lives. We expected air
raids every day and when the sirens sounded, we braced
ourselves for the worst.*

By the time Dad enrolled at Cardiff University, Britain had been at
war with Germany for at least a month. And Poland was now being
strangled by two immense powers. The Nazi–Soviet Non-Aggression
Pact agreed in August gave Hitler freedom to pursue his ambitions
without fear of reprisals from Russia. So on 17 September, as the pact
had set out, Russia invaded Poland from the east, crushing any Polish
resistance. The Warsaw government surrendered on 27 September.

John found digs in 2 Plasnewydd Place, in the Roath area of
the city. Along with two other ministerial students, Wynne Jones
and Elvet Cox, this would be his home for the next few years.

*Our landlady was a widow who was glad of the company but
I fear our behaviour as students wasn't always as charitable
as it could have been. One of the things we noticed from
the beginning was her use of gravy browning on her legs.
She drew straight lines at the back of her legs and smudged*

them with the brown colouring so as to give the appearance
of wearing stockings. We had never seen this before and it
provided us young men with endless amusement for a while.

From the end of September, rationing was introduced to Britain. In particular, petrol was rationed very carefully and only military personnel or people employed on government service were allowed petrol tokens. Depending on each person's place of work, each car was allowed between four and ten gallons of Pool (Standard) petrol per month at 1/6d per gallon.

Most people didn't have a car of course but the lack of
vehicles on the road suddenly became more apparent. And
on Sundays there were fewer buses and trains running, which
made it difficult to get to and from preaching appointments.
I had a friend called Trevor, whom I'd met in Baptist circles,
and he had some kind of top secret job with the government.
I never found out what he did; I'd assumed he was a bank
clerk until the war began. Trevor lived in a village called
Bedwas, a few miles east of Caerphilly. Whatever his role,
he had an endless supply of petrol and could go wherever
he wished. Dressed in civilian clothes, he was always being
stopped by army cordons, but waved on after they saw his
papers. But Trevor was a repository of stories; times when
his petrol had been siphoned off and he was stranded in
the mountains of mid Wales and had to wait for an army
lorry to drive him to a garage. I'm sure he once said he was
mistaken for a German spy and ended up in the cells for a
few hours. But many were the times when he gave me a lift
to various preaching engagements on Sunday as part of his
"government" duties!

One of John's flatmates, Elvet Cox, was an old friend from his days in Ilston and Trefeca. Wynne Jones had come straight to university from grammar school in Monmouthshire. All three of them were devastated by the turn of events and at the failure of diplomacy, and their conversations were dominated by the war.

> We'd sit up into the early hours discussing politics and the impact of war on the country. The other two seemed to me to be rather woolly in their thinking and I saw it as my job to promote the cause of non-violent protest. The more aerated I became, the more Wynne sucked on his pipe until we had to open the windows to let the smoke out! Despite my outspoken comments, Wynne's influence on me was probably the greatest as I took up smoking cigarettes for a while!

In that period, the BD (Bachelor Divinity) degree was a postgraduate course and so my father had to complete an initial degree in Philosophy whilst also studying at the South Wales Baptist College in Cardiff's Richmond Road. Established in the city in 1893, it had previously been situated in Pontypool after its beginnings in Abergavenny. By the time John arrived, nonconformist Christianity in Wales still had its share of bustling and well-attended chapels; although there was decline. The collapse of religious confidence after the First World War and the searching questions posed by evolutionary science had drained the faithful of zeal and numbers.

CHAPTER 11

1939, Cardiff 9050

It's a dark red, slim notebook with pages torn out. On the cover in a patented handwriting font are the words Memo Book. On the inside cover is the name of the first owner of this small pad, before it came into the possession of my father. The first owner's name was Gerald Griffiths, and his address is given as S.W.B.C. Gerald was a fellow student at South Wales Baptist College who later had churches in Edinburgh, South Africa, and finally Canada. I remember Gerald and his wife Kitty visiting us in about 1973 and felt in awe of them. Even though he had been brought up in the valleys, he had a kind of transatlantic sheen about him, at least to my teenage eyes. Whereas my dad's health was beginning to fail and his asthma attacks were becoming a daily feature, Gerald looked strong and confident. His wife had her own well-known Christian radio show for children called *A Visit with Mrs G*. I'd forgotten about them until I read Gerald's name in this notebook. After the torn-out pages are my father's sermon notes written in Welsh. On the back inside cover, written by my father, are two names, the first placed within quotation marks: "Mr Preston". Underneath is another name and address: Miss Messenger, Supplementary Register, Ministry of Labour,

Dominions House, Queen Street. Underneath this is a short statement: "Put me on S.R." and a large smudgy arrow points to the aforementioned Supplementary Register. The penultimate row simply says "Friday" and the bottom line has a scrawled rectangle saying "9050".

Under the 1939 National Service Act, as we have seen, all men aged between eighteen and forty-one had to register at their nearest employment exchange. This step was compulsory, and only after this would men be separated for military service, exemption, or conscientious objection. Because of the high numbers anticipated, registration would only take place on appointed Saturdays and during the war there were thirty-nine registrations. In 1939, men aged between twenty and twenty-three were registered and those between twenty-three and thirty-five were registered in 1940. By June 1941, every eligible male within the scope of the Act had been registered. From 1941 onwards, unmarried women aged between twenty and forty-one were also required to register, the first time in Britain that women were called up for military service. They were not allowed to engage in combat but were allocated to one of the women's services such as the Women's Royal Naval Service (WRNS) and the Women's Land Army.

I had to register in the middle of September. I could have delayed until later in the year but I wanted to get it over with as soon as possible. My nearest employment exchange was the Ministry of Labour in Queen Street, in the city centre. It was a large building, probably the largest of its kind in the city. I walked down with Wynne and Elvet, and they were laughing as we walked. I was deep in thought. They seemed happy enough to declare that they were part of the clergy and thus exempt. I knew I had to do more than this, voice

*my protest in some way. By the time we arrived, I was feeling
very nervous and not a little sick. The place was teeming with
men our age; possibly hundreds of us. We had to queue up in
the main hall and wait for a place to become vacant at one
of the desks at the front. My turn came and I walked up to
the man who was waiting to take my details. I gave my name
and then said I wanted to register as a conscientious objector.
He didn't flinch or even look at me. He simply told me that in
that case I had to walk down the corridor and somebody else
would see to me.*

*By the time I reached the room he'd told me about I saw
a few familiar faces. Wynne, Elvet, a few of the boys from
college and plenty of others I didn't know. It seemed this was
where everyone came who had a reason not to fight; a place
where they processed your claim, gave you a form to fill in
and explained what would happen next.*

By 1945 a total of 8,355,500 men had been registered under the
Military Training Act. Out of this total nearly 60,000 had registered
as conscientious objectors. Many were expressing their religious
convictions, drawn from an eclectic array of orthodox Christian
denominations and beyond. Baptists, Quakers, Plymouth Brethren,
Methodists, Anglicans, Catholics, Congregationalists, Calvinistic
Methodists, Presbyterians, Independents, Christadelphians,
and Jehovah's Witnesses; all had members who refused to fight.
But conscience wasn't the preserve of the religious. Socialists,
anarchists, communists, and Welsh nationalists also tried to
register as conscientious objectors.

*I'd say the atmosphere in the room was more tense than
the one I'd been in earlier. It was smaller, packed and we*

all knew that this was where our battle began; our battle to be heard and exempted. It was the same system; you waited in line until a desk came available and then you were interviewed. I was given a form to fill, personal details and so on, and then another form on which I had to write a personal statement: my reasons for being excused from combat duty on the basis of conscience. I was told that I would need this when I came before a tribunal and the judge would assess my case on the basis of my argument. Just before I left, [the interviewer] asked me what I did for a living; I think he was just passing the time of day. When I replied that I was in training to be a church minister, he more or less snorted and told me I needn't bother filling any forms as I wouldn't need them. Clergy of all denominations and those training to be ministers were automatically exempt from military service. And then he rather patronisingly told me to go away and have a nice war. I stood my ground however and told him I already knew of this exemption and I wanted to voice my own individual protest against the war and be registered as a conscientious objector. I had complied with the law and gone on the national register and it was my right to be put on that register as a conscientious objector. My faith and understanding of the teachings of Christ forbade me from taking the life of another and this needed to be heard. I don't think he knew what to do with me so he advised me to complete the form and I would hear from the Ministry of Labour again in due course.

As I walked back to Plasnewydd Place I felt a sense of elation, a kind of joy. I knew I was doing the right thing and I had borne witness to Jesus Christ in a public setting.

At the beginning of November, John had a free weekend with no preaching and he decided to visit his parents back in Gorseinon. He wanted to see his family and in particular he felt the need to tell his parents about his decision to register as a conscientious objector.

On Saturday evening the house was quiet and the conversation turned naturally to the war. It was Dat who broached the subject of the national register as it reminded him of a similar register he had to sign in the Great War. It had prompted huge controversy at the time as people feared the State's motives. This was my perfect opening, but I felt I stammered and stumbled my way to explaining my decision. I had no idea how they would react, especially Dat. I knew he'd tried to sign up for military action during the Great War and I feared he might be disappointed in me. But I needn't have feared. He said that as a minister of the gospel I had no other choice than to seriously apply the Bible's injunctions not to take the life of another and to love others as I had been loved. Interestingly enough he also remarked that the First World War had made him disillusioned with global politics. "We were told it would be a short war and that we were fighting for all that was good and decent in the world. In all honesty no one knew what the war was about then and we're none the clearer now. It's left a legacy of huge poverty and unemployment and has led into another war."

Like other conscientious objectors, John was placed on a provisional list ahead of the tribunal hearing he would attend when notified. In the meantime he had to complete his personal statement, which needed to be sufficiently persuasive to convince a judge and two other lay people of his objection to military combat. As a student he also had his studies to attend to.

Settling into student life, John was invited to a meeting of the Student Christian Movement or SCM as it was known. The SCM was formed in 1889 as a federation of voluntary student Christian unions. Its main aim was the promotion of overseas missions and facilitating Christian students to pursue this as a vocation. Within a very short time its influence on mainstream church life was considerable, largely due to former members assuming prominent positions within their denominations and using SCM as a platform for ecumenical and theological dialogue. In 1910, the SCM helped facilitate the groundbreaking Edinburgh Missionary Conference. Chaired by the American J. R. Mott, a leader within the Student Volunteer Movement for Foreign Missions and the World Student Christian Federation, the conference called for greater cooperation leading to unity among the Protestant denominations. Confident in its ecumenism and the superiority of the Christian message above all others, this movement saw greater unity of church and nations as the inevitable trajectory of Western civilization. Charles Clayton Morrison, editor of *The Christian Century*, gave an eyewitness account of the mood of optimism present in the conference:

Everyone feels the presence in the conference of a power not ourselves, deeper than our own devices, which is making for a triumphant advance of Christianity abroad. And not less are the delegates thrilled by the sense that the conference foreshadows a new era for the church at home.[1]

The SCM's theological position reflected the bias of the major Protestant denominations which had been heavily influenced by the liberal approach to scholarship coming out of Germany. Sceptical of traditional approaches to biblical interpretation, this movement laid great emphasis on the ethical teaching of Christ, particularly expressed in the Sermon on the Mount and the idea of building the kingdom of God on earth.

The SCM in Cardiff was made up of people I knew very well indeed – in fact I lived with two of them! There were also a few students from the Baptist college and many others whom I didn't know. They were a happy and cheerful group and very active in supporting social projects. Quite a few of them helped with the homeless who tended to be found in the Docks area of the city. I felt quite at home among them, familiar with the people and literature that were quoted. Muriel Lester's name popped up, as did Kagawa's and Gandhi's. And even though Dick Sheppard had recently died, they spoke warmly about him and a number of them were also members of the Peace Pledge Union.

For that term, the war dominated the SCM's meetings. Most of us were pacifists and were delighted when the brilliant philosopher Bertrand Russell was invited to speak at the university about war. But I also felt undernourished by the SCM. Despite its emphasis on good works and world evangelisation, it seemed to me they had very little substance to them. I agreed with them wholeheartedly in their call for what they termed the social gospel and politically I was one of them. And yet there was no real Bible teaching and little confidence that the Bible had any real relevance to today's world. Jesus Christ was largely a figure of history, a man to emulate, with teachings to admire but essentially unknowable. My belief and experiences convinced me that

*faith was more than an intellectual game buoyed along by a
kind of mysticism.*

Before the year was out, John was made aware of another student
Christian group called the Inter Varsity Fellowship, or IVF. This
movement was launched in 1928 in reaction to the perceived
theological bias of the SCM. The IVF emphasized the infallibility
of the Bible as God's Word, the death of Christ being the only
means of making peace with God and personal evangelism. There
were only a small number of IVF groups in existence in British
universities at the time.

*It was a funny little group, much more earnest than the
SCM, and considerably smaller. They were very serious
about the Bible and a guest speaker was invited each week.
It was led by a woman, Mair Thomas, which was unusual in
those days. She was very self-assured and organised. I didn't
know what to make of her. I'm not sure we hit it off at first.
She probably thought I was a little woolly and I thought her
too direct!*

The IVF was inspired by Norman Grubb, a young Cambridge
University student who in 1919 sought to evangelize his college.
He had become disaffected with the SCM's doctrinal position on
various matters and by the late 1920s a number of other university
Christian unions had followed his example and functioned
independently of the SCM. The IVF's first general secretary
was Douglas Johnson, who led the organization to its formal
establishment in 1928. Since the late 1930s it had had a presence
in the University of South Wales and Monmouthshire in Cardiff.
A young scion of the Barclays banking family, Oliver Barclay,

was also making an impact on the movement and was recruiting a range of influential figures. These included a young Anglican priest, John Stott; and Dr Martyn Lloyd Jones, a physician turned church minister now on the staff at the prestigious Westminster Chapel, and who had had such a profound impact on Dat some years earlier. The builder Sir John Laing was drawn into the IVF's schemes to build a research centre in Cambridge, a sign of Barclay's important financial connections.

In December, John received a letter informing him of the tribunal he must attend. It would be held in March at the Ministry of Labour in Queen Street, the same address where he had registered. He was to appear before a bench of three officials: a county court judge, a trade unionist, and a doctor. He would be asked to read his personal statement and then address any questions arising from his statement. Failure to attend would breach the Military Service Act and could lead to a custodial sentence.

Even though I had had pacifist leanings since I was a teenager, I had never really presented a case for myself apart from my short presentation before the Cymrodorion. But I was considerably younger then and also I was mainly showing off about the number of books I'd read at that tender age. Where would I start with my defence? I was inclined again to start with my literary heroes: Tolstoy, Gandhi and Kagawa. I thought of some of Donald Soper's words I'd come across in a radio broadcast: "You never cast out evil by evil. You can't conquer violence by more violence, or fear by terror." But this was unsatisfactory; this had to be my statement and not somebody else's. My starting place had to be the central message of Christianity: the love

*of God towards his enemies, humanity, in the death and
resurrection of Jesus Christ. There you have it, I thought.
Everything flows out from this crucial message of grace.
Several Bible verses flooded my mind. God was in Christ
reconciling the world to himself. Whilst we were still sinners
Christ died for the ungodly. God loves his enemies, Jesus
told us to love our enemies and, when faced with assault, we
should turn the other cheek. So I based my entire defence on
my understanding of the Christian gospel, Bible references
included, concluding that as a Christian I could not
contradict the Bible and kill another human being.*

When the day of the hearing arrived, John was at peace with
himself:

*I was well prepared; more than that I was convinced of the
rightness of my cause. Like Martin Luther, I felt I could say to
the bench, "Here I stand: I can do no other."*

On arrival at the Ministry of Labour, he was taken to a waiting
room. It was full of men waiting for their hearings and the air was
thick with cigarette smoke.

*The mood was tense and my peace of mind which had
seemed so strong half an hour earlier now seemed fragile.
We were all in the same boat and my voice would be one
of many. I was finally called into the board room and I had
to stand at a table which faced a row of three men seated.
Behind me were other people and this took me by surprise.
Some of them were the general public but there were also
some newspaper reporters taking notes. Anxiety overtook*

*me; the immense reality of what I was about to do. I was
going to disagree with the government in public and I felt
very small indeed. Before reading my statement I had to give
my name, address and occupation. When I explained that
I was studying to be a Baptist minister, the chairman of the
bench got very exasperated with me.*

*"You are wasting our time, young man. You must know,
as well as the next man, that members of the clergy are
automatically exempt from military service. You are not a
conscientious objector, so please explain what you are doing
in front of us today."*

*I didn't want to add to the man's ill temper but I told
him that I objected strongly to warfare on the grounds that
it was immoral and against the basic tenets of Christianity.
I also reminded him that I was a student and not a minister
so the exemption probably didn't apply to me. I could see he
was going to dismiss me from the room, so I asked if I might
read out my statement. This I was allowed to do and then
I was asked a few questions. The trade unionist asked me if
I'd even read the Old Testament as there were any number
of wars recorded in its pages. The judge had clearly lost all
interest in my presence and accused me of being naive and
selective in my use of the Bible. I felt a flash of indignation
and told him that if he knew his Bible at all he would come
to the same conclusion as me. Thankfully he wasn't enraged
and concluded by saying that I had successfully presented
my case and I would be registered as a conscientious
objector. Since I was eager to be known as a conscientious
objector he hoped I wouldn't object to providing valuable
service to the community. I said I would be only too happy
to serve provided it didn't imply any acceptance of the war*

effort on my part. He seemed to find this amusing. "Thank you, reverend; you'll be contacted again regarding your service soon."

Within a week I received a letter again from a Mr Norton asking me to come for an appointment to be placed on the supplementary register for community service. The appointment would be next Friday with Miss Messenger and would I confirm by either visiting the Ministry of Labour or telephoning Cardiff 9050.

CHAPTER 12

1940, Air Raid Warden

This is a press cutting, thin, yellow-stained, and torn paper, dated 22 November 1939:

Disillusioned Peace Forces

"The peace forces find themselves in a discouraged mood," says *The Christian Century* (Chicago). "For a dozen years the peace movement grew in optimism. During the past four years it has been seized with a sense of frustration. And during the past two years it has been more difficult to keep the fires burning than at any time since 1918. There is everywhere talk of war."

The nations have not in fifty years been in such a state of nerves with respect to one another as today... For a dozen years we lived in a post war mood. Today we are living in a pre war mood. We are no longer looking back at a World War – we are looking forward to another World War. There has come upon the mind of the world, including many of the most ardent peace advocates, a deep sense of disillusionment with respect to all that has been done... Is peace still a dream?

In my assorted collection of papers, notebooks, diaries, and photographs, there are a number of press cuttings: pages torn out from national, local, and religious newspapers folded and used by Dad as bookmarks. Due to their age and the draughty garage in which they were kept, most of them are faded, fragile, and smell of damp. This one dates back to the early weeks of the war and comes from *The British Weekly*, a religious newspaper aimed at Christians in nonconformist (non-Anglican or Catholic) churches. The writer is quoting from an American religious periodical, *The Christian Century*, published in Chicago. In 1939 America had yet to enter the war, and it was by no means obvious that it would do so, which explains the discussion of a possible future world war. But my attention is drawn to another observation: the apparent failure of the peace movement. It was hoped that World War One would be the war to end all wars, a catchphrase coined originally by H. G. Wells and made famous by President Woodrow Wilson. With the creation of the League of Nations in 1920, there was a real anticipation that international disagreements could be resolved peaceably without resorting to armed conflict. Through better education and the advancement of science, surely war would be a thing of the past? This was the period when the Peace Pledge Union was founded and when peace campaigners such as Muriel Lester, Donald Soper, Bertrand Russell, and others promoted the pacifist cause. But Germany's aggression and the subsequent declarations of war made by European nations signalled the failure of the peace movement. *The Christian Century*, and presumably *The British Weekly*, opined that the dream of peace was collapsing like a house of cards.

Just before Christmas 1939, John returned to the Ministry of Labour to meet with Miss Messenger:

I felt quite relaxed about this meeting; after all, I had done the hard part and faced the tribunal. How wrong I was! Miss Messenger was a lady in her late 30s and she didn't smile once during our appointment. Her manner was brusque, distant and disapproving. From the time I was shown into her office I could tell that she was not impressed with me. As someone who was now exempt from military service, I was to serve the country by performing supplementary war duties. In my case I would become an air raid warden. I was to report to my local unit on City Road, where I would be allocated a uniform and given my orders. I tried to make contact and engineered a handshake as I left but she would have nothing to do with it.

John went home to his parents in Gorseinon for Christmas; a rather tense affair as people expected the artificial silence of the phoney war to break at any moment:

The atmosphere was rife with rumours of one sort or another. There was talk of a surprise German parachute invasion that had taken place and they were blending in as locals. Some of them were even dressed up as monks apparently!

When he arrived in Brynhyfryd Road, however, he discovered another resident:

When I went into the living room, there was a girl sitting down completely unknown to me. I assumed she was a neighbour's child but I soon found out her real identity. She was an evacuee from London and along with her school, had been sent to Gorseinon in case London was bombed.

Mam and Dat seemed to be enjoying having her to stay but how they all understood each other I do not know. She had a pronounced cockney accent which seemed harsh and glottal compared to my parents' lilting Carmarthenshire speech. But we all got on well and enjoyed a good Christmas. The press and radio coverage was however dominated by the threat of an imminent German attack.

But there was no attack and the phoney war continued. Early in the spring term of 1940, John reported for duty as an air raid warden and was given his uniform:

The unit to which I belonged was situated in someone's front room on City Road! He was an older man, Mr Jefferies was his name, and he'd fought in the First World War. He was a friendly, courteous man and not once did he ask me about my views on war. He did however insist on calling me Rev on every occasion. There was a crucifix hanging up on his front room wall so I imagine he must have been a Roman Catholic. I was given a tin hat with a capital W on the front to signal my status as an air raid warden. I had a whistle to blow when my authority had to be asserted and a long grey coat for the cold nights. More disturbingly I was also handed a gas mask and anti gas suit to wear in case of an attack. Even though I was on the supplementary register, I now felt that I was part of the war effort. Whatever my views were, I was charged with keeping people safe and dealing with any bombs that might fall on my patch. It was a sobering realisation.

Before Prime Minister Chamberlain declared war on Germany on 3 September 1939, blackout regulations had come into force.

During night hours, measures had to be taken by all householders and business owners to ensure that no light whatsoever was visible from the outside of their properties. Car lights were adapted so that beams shone downwards and there was a blanket ban on all street lights.

I had to work 24 hours a week, mostly from 8pm to 4am. We went around in pairs, normally with the same person. I was partnered with another university student. There was something magical about the city during those night hours. There was barely anyone around and all the buildings looked empty because of the blackout. The lack of street lighting gave the streets an eerie, a kind of haunted atmosphere. On a quiet night I often thought about my family back in Gorseinon, and prayed that they would be kept well and safe.

Air raid wardens had to ensure that people knew how to get to their nearest shelters without any delay:

To start with, particularly in the early months of 1940, the air raid sirens sounded sometimes several times a day and night. Against my character, I had to badger and hector people and blow my whistle if I felt they were dragging their feet. The atmosphere was generally good humoured, although once or twice someone would tell me to get a proper job and go and fight. Occasionally there was panic, but very rarely; people seemed to take it in their stride. Children, especially at night, could get disoriented but there were beds for them all and I think they quite liked the sense of being together with everyone they knew.

It was a year of new beginnings for John. His attendance at the IVF grew in frequency, attracted as he was by the group's emphasis on the Bible and theology. He was also a little more than interested in Mair Thomas who led the group. Despite a few innocent flirtations in summer schools, John had never been seriously romantically involved with anyone, but he felt drawn to her.

At first, she seemed very suspicious of me. I don't know why; maybe because I was training to be a minister and she thought I wasn't "sound" in my views. It could have been that she noticed I smoked, although in reality it was a very irregular habit. It was probably because the first time I went to the IVF I was being jocular and light hearted, largely to get her attention. It clearly didn't work the first time around!

What struck me in those meetings was their certainty of faith. There was an emphasis on having your own faith, of coming to faith, which they called "conversion". It reminded me of the way I responded to David Shepherd's preaching when I was a teenager and how I experienced the love and forgiveness of God personally. There was a warmth in the way they prayed and a real belief that God would answer. The meetings were in English which was strange to me. Even though I was fully bilingual, Welsh was the language of faith and chapel. The hymns that were sung in the IVF were all in English, some I knew and others I didn't. It wasn't just the language that was different; the culture of the group was quite unlike anything I'd experienced before. I remember asking Mair once why there was so little Welsh in the meetings, particularly as it was our mother tongue. She said that the most important reason for the IVF's existence was to spread the gospel so that people would hear and follow

Christ. Everything else was subordinate to this main aim. Discussion and debate were encouraged, although there was this tremendous clarity about the authority of the Bible.

It was through the IVF I started reading literature from a very different theological stable to my own: the English Puritans, Calvin's Institutes, Spurgeon's sermons and JC Ryle. And once a month an eminent guest speaker would come and address us and we were encouraged to invite all our friends to come and listen. I especially remember being stirred by listening to men like Arnold Aldis, a consultant surgeon who had recently come to teach in the city's Royal Infirmary. He had come from University College Hospital, London, and he was an amazing speaker. He brought the Bible alive to me and his faith in Christ was sincere and winsome. Another electrifying speaker was Arthur Rendle Short, a professor of surgery at Bristol University. Like Dr Aldis, he spoke clearly and simply of the need to know Christ for yourself. These were brilliant men, outstanding in their own fields and yet not ashamed to preach a message that was simple enough for anyone to understand. And whenever we had a guest speaker, there was always an appeal for people to become Christians. And they did! I had never seen this sort of thing happen so regularly before. So the numbers at the meetings started growing and growing.

Another regular speaker was Dr Martyn Lloyd Jones. After leading a church in Aberavon, Lloyd Jones was now assistant minister in London's prestigious Westminster Chapel. With a reputation for austerity and seriousness, he had gained a reputation for his Bible teaching, and large crowds gathered to hear him. His national impact on the IVF was considerable, but my father's feelings towards him were ambivalent:

He was a very fine speaker and very clear in his teaching.
He had immersed himself in the scriptures and quoted
freely from the Puritans. But there was this exclusivity I
found difficult. He seemed to be opposed to all the main
denominations and regularly made jibes about the liberalism
of the Baptists in particular. I found it offensive and had
more than one difference of opinion with him.

As his involvement with the IVF grew, so John's association with the SCM weakened. He was making a choice about the kind of Christianity he favoured and it took him away from his own roots. There must have been conflict for him in this decision. The basis for his pacifism had come from writers and activists endorsed by the SCM. Donald Soper, Muriel Lester, and Dick Sheppard were all Christians whose passion for peace was rooted in the Bible, although their interpretation of its contents would have been more radical than the conservative outlook of the IVF. Up to this point he'd been influenced by campaigners, people who'd sought to change things. Starved of meaningful relationships with like-minded COs, Dad's sense of social justice was likely to go inward as he embraced the more pietistic paths of Calvinistic Christianity.

In a sermon called "Why Does God Allow War?"[1], preached in 1939, Martyn Lloyd Jones offered his assessment of the causes of war. In essence, he saw it as a symptom of humanity's sin and the only remedy was faith in Christ. Campaigning for peace and a better world was superficial, since the real problems lay within the human heart and not in governmental change. Another sermon, preached in 1963 from a verse in Galatians, also illustrated his view of pacifism and pacifists:

I have to say, in order to be honest and to be plain, that some of the most bitter men I have ever met in my life have been pacifists. I have never seen such bitter hatred in the hearts of men.[2]

Dad was heavily influenced by Martyn Lloyd Jones and maybe this explains why he had so little to say about his pacifist views during and immediately after the war. Could it be that he feared meeting the disapproval of a man he admired and a group he had recently joined? As he embarked on a new adventure in terms of his Christianity, I can't help feeling that a light was being turned off in his own mind at least for the time being.

Looking back at this period in his life, this is how John surveyed it in 1983:

> When I went up to the university, the SCM seemed preoccupied with practical issues to the exclusion of doctrine, while in the IVF – although this was to change under the influence of Martyn Lloyd Jones – there was a tendency towards pietism that wasn't much concerned with social or moral matters, despite the fact that we were in the throes of the Second World War...

But Dad was not comfortable in clubs, associations, or networks. Just as his conscientious objection was largely a personal matter, so too with his later church ministry. He would remain within the Baptist Union of churches but never assumed any particular seniority within the denomination. And ironically, when Martyn Lloyd Jones called for ministers to leave their denominations and join the new Evangelical Movement of Wales, John refused and publicly disagreed with him. At heart I think he needed the freedom to think for himself and baulked instinctively at any kind of herd instinct.

This was a strange period in terms of the war's progression. Once Germany and Russia had invaded Poland in September 1939, there followed a kind of hiatus for eight months: the so-called phoney war referred to earlier. But this changed dramatically on 10 May 1940, when the German troops started to roll westwards, invading Belgium, Luxembourg, and the Netherlands, and entered France. Attempts by the British Expeditionary Force and other Allied troops to stem this advance failed, and soon 350,000 troops had retreated to the Channel coast and were awaiting certain defeat. But the German forces were halted at Hitler's express command. Speculation still surrounds the reason behind this strange order, but it meant that for three days, from 28 May, the UK government dispatched thirty-nine large ships and destroyers to rescue most of the stranded troops, although this was done under heavy gunfire from the German planes. This rescue operation is also remembered for the 800-strong flotilla of pleasure craft, fishing boats, and merchant marine boats that crossed the English Channel. Most of the troops were brought over to England, although tens of thousands had lost their lives in the Battle of France, and many others were marched off to German prisoner of war camps.

Just before midnight at the end of June 1940, air raid sirens boomed across Cardiff signalling possible German attack. It turned out to be a Luftwaffe spying mission. On 9 July, a bomber flying over the docks struck a ship carrying timber, killing seven of the crew. Towards the end of August, the Splott area of the city was bombed, and some residents in Portmanmoor Road, Crighton Street, North Street, and Homfray Street were injured or killed. In September there were further bombing attacks on the city. Homes in Arabella Street, Moy Road, and Woodville Road were demolished, with loss of life. The Cardiff ice house in the docks (used for storing imported meat and fruit) was gutted, as was the Tresilian Hotel. The war had arrived in Cardiff.

From the summer onwards I was frantically busy. The combination of university work, travelling around the churches of South Wales and air raid duties meant I was flat out all the time. I didn't go home that summer; I couldn't, due largely to the increased bombing over the city. With the bombs, came fear. You could almost smell it and taste it. No amount of routine could delete the sense that we were under attack and there was a real anticipation that there was worse to come. We were all too aware that the coal which was exported to the world from Cardiff docks made the city a perfect target. It was surely only a matter of time before we had a real taste of German firepower.

John and Mair's involvement with the IVF (John was now on the committee) meant that they saw a great deal of each other. Planning, organizing, praying, evangelizing; in short they were being evangelically busy. There was a depth developing between them beyond shared projects and passions; they were beginning to find love.

We had much in common; we had very little in common. We were both Welsh speakers and came from areas of heavy industry. We were steeped in eisteddfodau and chapel culture and yet were so different. Whereas I had seen my parents battle with want and insufficiency, Mair's family kept a maid. I had had to leave school in order to support my family, but Mair had matriculated, studied at a missionary college in London for two years, and was studying for a degree in Music. And all of it paid for by her father. Mair's mother however had died when she was only in her teens and she felt her absence very keenly.

Whilst her mother was dying, Mair stayed with a family in Aberystwyth. Through their example and being taken to some meetings in the town, she became a Christian. In this our stories were very similar. But Mair's understanding of that experience was far sharper than my own. As far as she was concerned, the moment she chose to follow Christ was the turning point of her life. A line had been drawn between what she had been and what she would be. When I spoke of my experience, she challenged me along the same lines. I think she felt that I saw it as a continuation of a previously held faith, a kind of spiritual development. She would have none of it. "You were born again on that night, and it's a complete break with the religion you knew before." My time in the IVF had already convinced me of this but she lost no time in letting me know her opinion.

Her time in London intrigued me. I still had yet to leave Wales, let alone visit London, and her stories sounded like a faraway place. Her tales of conducting open air meetings in the East End and working with the Jews created a very strong impression that this was a woman on her way to save the world – singlehandedly if needs be! She was amazing. She'd been to an all women college [Mount Hermon] that trained church leaders for work overseas; I didn't know that such an establishment existed until I met Mair. And here she was leading the IVF in Cardiff; again it was unheard of for women to be in such leadership. But she took it all in *her stride, even the criticism that came her way. From time to time, particularly from visiting speakers, there would come jibes about women leadership, but generally she kept her counsel. She was confident in her gifts, believed she was doing what God wanted her to do and simply got on with it. And in fairness to her, she was not a tyrannical chair. She formed a committee, delegated responsibility and led the team. However, she knew her mind and at times could be very sharp with people who crossed the line. There was one occasion when someone goaded her about women in leadership and she snapped that instead of worrying about other people's lives, he should get on with his own. That was the beginning and end of the conversation!*

On the subject of war we were divided. She took the view that when the government declared war on Germany, all other means for peace had been exhausted. It was up to Christians, like everyone else, to support the government and fight if needs be. She was however sympathetic to my argument, particularly as my reasoning came out of my understanding of the Bible's teaching on the matter. Our discussions would sometimes go long into the night but, like a few other things, we agreed to disagree!

As the year drew to a close, this 22-year-old had opened the door to two influential voices which would shape the rest of his days. His Christianity from 1940 onwards was dominated by the ideas and writings of Reformed theology, with its emphasis on the works of John Calvin and the Puritans. Gone now the ecumenical and inclusive leanings of the SCM, replaced by the black and white certainties of evangelicalism. But the greatest influence was Mair. As with the other strong women in John's life, he needed her certainty and clarity. His inclinations were towards open-ended discussion but he was ineluctably drawn to someone who knew her mind and in this he felt safe.

Looking back at his experiences in 1940, I see brushstrokes of the man I knew decades later. Throughout his life my dad promoted the evangelical faith both inside and outside the pulpit. He was very clear about innate human wickedness and the need to experience God's forgiveness personally, through faith in Jesus. Publicly he could at times be critical of other denominations and divergent theological viewpoints, but privately he was often more nuanced and accommodating. To the end of his life he retained a deep love for tutors and ministerial colleagues whose opinions were very different to his own, in part I believe because he envied their freedom to think beyond the theological box in which he found himself. Like many a soldier caught in battle, he found himself in no man's land.

CHAPTER 13

An Appointment in London

Here I have a black ebony cane with an ivory horn-shaped handle, and a silver band wrapped around the top of the cane underneath the handle. It was given to Dat as a commemorative gift for his part in founding the union branch at the Grovesend Tin Works in Gorseinon. The silver plate has long since disappeared but as I recall as a child reading the oval-shaped plate with the commendation inscription. It still strikes me as an unusual gift for a union member. Its expense was a recognition of his efforts in promoting the rights of his workers but it's the kind of accessory more associated with men of wealth. Something more likely to have been used by Burlington Bertie than Thomas the tin. It's now in my home and when I look at it, I imagine someone walking grandly down the Strand complete with long coat and top hat.

After his industrial accident, Dat found it difficult to walk with confidence and this stick became his support. When he died in 1958, the walking stick was given to my dad, kept in numerous cloakrooms, and remained unused until he was afflicted by blindness in his late seventies. As with his own father before him, the stick steadied his feet. It reminds me of Dad's faltering steps in his last years and provokes me to think of him walking gingerly around the blacked out city of Cardiff.

In December 1940, Cardiff was braced for attack:

I was already back in Cardiff after a very short Christmas break. In fact I was only home for Christmas Eve, Christmas Day and Boxing Day. It was a strange experience; it was the first time ever that we didn't go to church on Christmas Day. Noddfa, in fact all the churches and chapels, didn't open. I had the impression that there had been some sort of edict pronounced, preventing crowds of people walking to church and drawing the attention of the enemy.

There was tension everywhere. As though something was about to snap over the country. Even though the Battle of Britain in the skies had ended, we knew that the war was still in its early stages. I feared that worse times were ahead. Back in Cardiff my landlady called us down to her parlour towards the end of December. She sounded anxious and was eager for us to hear a news item. In a grave tone of voice, the broadcaster announced that London was sustaining a barrage of bombing from incendiary devices and many parts of the city were now on fire. Many of the city's oldest buildings were ruined and thousands of homes were in flames. He said that it was too early to say how much permanent damage had been caused but it was already being referred to as the second great fire of London.

The bombing continued throughout the night and into the early hours of the morning, stretching from Islington to the graveyard of St Paul's Cathedral. More than 24,000 high-explosive bombs and 100,000 incendiary devices were dropped on the city and around

160 people killed with hundreds injured on this one night alone. The timing of the blitzkrieg had been carefully coordinated to coincide with low tide on the Thames, making it difficult to pump the water needed to diffuse the 1,500 fires started. Amazingly, despite the carnage wrought on much of the square mile of London, Christopher Wren's greatest surviving masterpiece, St Paul's, escaped another fire.

At the beginning of the following day's air raid shift, an official briefing note was read out. It said that intelligence had been received of further imminent attacks against British cities and we were to be fully prepared to deal with the situation and cooperate fully with other services. We should expect casualties and ensure civil order at all times. My stomach turned as I heard this stark warning. Up to that point, there had been a few random attacks and dummy runs. We were now facing aggression of a different order.

The Cardiff skies were quiet for the next few nights. It seemed like a return to the phoney war until the evening of 2 January:

I was on duty and my ears were straining for the slightest unusual noise. The streets were quiet, no one was around and no traffic. Suddenly the siren wailed into the silence and the process began of ushering people to the shelters. That night the people were on edge and scared. We all knew that this was no run through; something was going to happen tonight. And then, maybe an hour or so later, there was a rumble in the air followed by a roar. It was a clear, cold night and you could see the dark planes silhouetted against the sky, like locusts. Curiously, just when the planes must have been over the city, it went eerily silent again. And then they fell and there was a horrid sensation. Not just the deafening, whistling, screaming sound they made but you could feel them land. The bottom end of City Road was only a mile or so away from Riverside and the vibrations carried. Windows rattled, and there was the grinding kind of feeling coming up from the ground. The explosions lit up the night air; at one time it felt as though the whole city was under attack. We kept waiting, expecting the worst to happen in our streets. I shall never forget the sounds and sights of that night. Those incendiary bombs were deadly but strangely beautiful. They seemed to scream towards their destination and then explode on contact; and the explosion generated was dazzling and multi coloured. For a few moments it was bright, and seemed like daylight even though it was pitch black.

It was a long and frightening night. At about three in the morning, a messenger arrived from the Grangetown area; there was need for extra manpower due to the severity of the bombing. Buildings were on fire and any number of people trapped inside or wandering around shocked. My father and a few others were dispatched to the scene.

We walked briskly through the quiet city streets, our eyes fixed at the fire work display above us. Down Queen Street, High Street, Clare Road and into Grangetown. The Baptist church in Clive Street was untouched but there were flames everywhere. I felt so helpless looking at these torched homes. Vainly the firemen tried to douse the flames but the heat was overwhelming. Someone told us to herd up the large numbers of displaced people and take them to safety in

nearby shelters. They were terrified, in great shock. As we
neared one house that was aflame, we heard the sound of
screaming from inside; they were being rescued but the sound
of frightened desperation made me want to be sick. What I
saw and heard that night confirmed to me the dehumanising
evil of warfare. These were innocent victims of war caused by
political leaders unable to negotiate with each other.

The capital's docks were among the busiest in the world and a vital supply line of coal, steel, and tin for the war effort. It was not the port however that bore the brunt of this attack but other densely populated areas. The districts of Canton, Riverside, and Grangetown were targeted, with considerable loss of life and damage to buildings. A stray bomb also struck Llandaff Cathedral. In total that night witnessed the death of 165 people, with a further 427 injured in the attack. Nearly 350 homes were destroyed in the frenzy and fifty people killed in Riverside's De Burgh Street alone.

As the year progressed, John's relationship with Mair took a surprising twist. Their war was about to become personal:

We hadn't seen each other properly for a few weeks, largely
attributable to my air raid duties and a number of preaching
engagements. When finally we did manage to go for a cup of
tea she gave me some surprising news. It seemed as though
she'd been contacted by someone in the Foreign Office and
more or less told to apply for a post in somewhere called
Bletchley Park. Mair had little information about this
place, except she thought it was somewhere in London and
was obviously a government department. The man who
approached her had told her that her linguistic skills would
be very useful in the fight against Germany, but beyond

that she knew very little. This government official gave her a name and address and in the strongest terms suggested she apply as soon as possible.

My reactions were very mixed I must say. I felt a little annoyed that Mair was going to be part of the war machine, part of the establishment. We differed in our views about pacifism but I suppose it hadn't occurred to me that Mair might somehow be involved in the war.

From spring 1941 onwards, as we have seen, single women between the ages of twenty and thirty were initially asked to enrol on a national register and by the end of the year compulsory conscription was mandated. Women were not allowed to take part in any military combat but served in a number of different capacities and organizations. Agriculture, forestry, ambulance duties, and working in munitions factories were among the more regular designations. However, Mair's approach by the Foreign Office predated the national register; she was part of a secret recruitment strategy.

But my real feelings weren't of a political nature. Mair's announcement disquieted me in a different way. What had begun as a friendship within a wider group was changing. We shared the same faith, the same passion for the gospel, and a growing sense of serving together in some way. But her announcement caught me off guard. The thought of being apart from each other and how the course of the war might affect us made me see things rather differently. I didn't reveal these feelings to Mair; I didn't think it would be fair or helpful. Nevertheless I was unsettled.

Mair's application resulted in a speedy invitation to attend an interview at the Foreign Office in Whitehall. She was given expenses to cover the railway journey and she asked John to accompany her to London. This would be his first visit to London:

I was filled with excitement at the prospect of this trip. I had to gain permission from my university and Baptist college tutors. I also arranged to work a different air raid shift that week. On the day we left Cardiff for London, I was wearing my best suit normally reserved for Sundays. I didn't want to let Mair down as she fraternised with posh government officials and if I'm to be honest I wanted to create a good impression on Mair.

We arrived in London with plenty of time to spare, a couple of hours in fact. Mair really knew her way around the city, thanks to her time in Mount Hermon. We took a bus to St Paul's cathedral and the evidence of the blitz was everywhere. Parts of Cardiff had been badly damaged but nothing like this. There was dereliction and rubble everywhere you looked. Somehow or another people were out and about and there was plenty of traffic, but it was a war zone. Mair was clearly moved by all this. She remembered a thriving, bustling city but here was a place brought to its knees. We got off at St Paul's and I remembered a photograph I'd seen in the Daily Mail, *taken during the Blitz. Not my newspaper of choice by any means due to its right wing leanings, but it was a most striking picture. It showed the cathedral rising majestically into the night sky of London above the rubble and flames. And stepping into St Paul's, I felt a sense of awe and mystery that was overpowering. It was a house of prayer and I found myself silently thanking*

God for his presence and provision. We had many lovely and simple chapels back home but this was special. Like Jacob in the book of Genesis, I found myself saying "This is none other than the house of God."

Despite the sense of devastation everywhere, I was entranced by London. I had never seen so many elegant and grand buildings, especially when we arrived in Whitehall. Whilst Mair went into the Foreign Office I went for a stroll along the Thames with the Houses of Parliament nearby and St Paul's in the distance. I thought of the pacifists I knew who had associations with the city: the late Dick Sheppard who served in St Martin in the Fields; Donald Soper who was at the West London Mission and Muriel Lester's community in the East End. Of course there was also Martyn Lloyd Jones, newly appointed to the Westminster Chapel, only a matter of minutes from where I was standing. He wouldn't have seen eye to eye with any of them!

John and Mair said very little to each other on the way home. Mair was deep in her thoughts, processing her experiences at the Foreign Office:

We hardly spoke and I didn't want to create further tension. Something had disturbed her at the Foreign Office and I would wait until she was ready to talk about it. When we arrived back in Cardiff, Mair wanted to see her father in Pontycymer and she was keen that I went with her. The silence was fairly unbearable; I confess that I thought our relationship might be over before it had really begun. But almost as soon as we arrived at her home, Mair burst into tears and it all came out. Not only had she been offered

*a post and accepted it, she had also signed the Official
Secrets Act. This was the thing that disturbed her more than
anything else. Before signing, it had been impressed on Mair
that she would be bound to secrecy for the rest of her days.
It forbade her from telling anyone about her work, almost
at pain of death. The penalties for disobedience were spelt
out and these included imprisonment. She felt conflicted;
excited that she'd been offered an exciting job but unhappy
that she couldn't tell us about any of it. She was so upset I did
the most instinctive thing – I took her hand and suggested
we prayed. I'm not entirely sure what I said but holding
her hand in that moment indicated that this had drawn us
together and not apart. Whatever happened now, I felt sure
that we would be together.*

At this moment, none of them, including Mair, knew what would
be achieved at Bletchley Park or what its purpose was. They felt
assured it was probably in London and had an important role to
play in the war. More than that, it was shrouded in mystery. Within
a matter of months, Mair graduated and headed for Bletchley
Park, which she learned was the name of a country house in
Buckinghamshire now used by the Foreign Office. For the time
being, she kept this a secret from John.

With Mair's departure, John was catapulted into the leadership
of the IVF. He had barely been part of the group for six months,
but his prominence was recognized by the rest of the group.
Looking back on Mair's presidency in his 1983 diary, this was his
assessment of her impact on the students:

*When I began my studies in Cardiff University in 1939, she
was the President of the CU (Christian Union) and remained*

*in post for a further year, giving incredible leadership to
a somewhat dispirited group. There was a real renewal
during her presidency and the whole nature of the CU was
transformed – it grew in numbers, in faith, in witnessing
power and for the first time became a force in the university.*

In the same entry, he recognized that his own theological understanding owed more to the IVF than to anything he had previously known:

*My debt to the IVF is incalculable and whatever theological
awareness I have is due more to their influences than to
anything I received through formal ministerial training. That
is not to decry my tutors at the Baptist college, for whom I had
a great affection, but their approach to theological study was
pretty unexciting and unadventurous. It was through the IVF
that my beliefs were crystallised and my convictions confirmed.
It opened my eyes to the importance of a daily walk with God
and the need for consistent living and fearless witness.*

But what was happening to this Conchie? He arrived at university just as war was declared and went out of his way to register as a CO. Where now was that idealism, that eagerness to change the world? He had been a young man so inspired by a vision of God's kingdom on earth that he identified with some of the most radical and progressive ideas about non-violent protest. Where was that young man now? I wonder whether, if the war against Germany had been declared six months later, his decision might have been different. Or rather he might have expressed himself differently. Maybe he would have simply hidden behind the exemption for clergy. The group he had joined had brought spiritual renewal but at the expense of the campaigning spirit that drove him to appear before the tribunal.

But surely this can't be right. He may have changed his theology but he was not swapping it for a machine gun. Decades later in his 1983 diary I can still hear his anti-establishment suspicion as a 64-year-old commenting on Thatcher's Conservative government's refusal to talk to CND (Campaign for Nuclear Disarmament) who were campaigning at Greenham Common:

A marvellous comment from the beloved "Tarzan" of the Conservative Party, Michael Heseltine, the Defence Secretary. In a speech to the Tories of Newbury – only a short distance away from the US base in Greenham Common, which has been besieged by thousands of women protesting against the threat to house nuclear missiles there – he explained why he had rejected engaging in public debate with the President of CND. He said "the unilateral mind of CND is closed to the multilateralism of the government." He might just have honestly said that the multilateral thinking of the government is closed to the unilateralism of CND. But no! It's the other people who have closed minds. We honest, sincere, rational Tories have minds that are open and untrammelled by the prejudices of lesser mortals! How easy it is to recognise the closed mind in others while failing to see it in ourselves.

This doesn't sound like a man who has rolled over and lost his social conscience. During the autumn, John received a cryptic summons from Professor T. W. Chance, principal of the South Wales Baptist College. An urgent message for John had been received by the college, and he was not at liberty to reveal its contents until they met: "Please come and see me urgently."

John's mind was alive with apprehension. What kind of missive was this? Had something happened to his parents? Was he in some sort of trouble?

As I made my way from the university to the Baptist college, walking – almost running – down Richmond Road, I feared the worst. Maybe I misinformed the Ministry of Labour about something and would find myself in prison or worse, forced to enlist as a soldier? Oh the shame I would bring on my parents and family!

His assessment was wrong, as Principal Chance explained:

"John, the college has been contacted by the Foreign Office but nothing for you to worry about. It concerns your good friend Mair Thomas who is also one of their employees. It transpires that Miss Thomas has been taken poorly with influenza and needs to return home for some convalescence. She is greatly weakened by her condition and she has specifically asked that you accompany her home. The Foreign Office has acceded to her wish and you are to meet her tomorrow by train and bring her home. All your travel and meal expenses will be fully met; these you will receive tomorrow at Cardiff railway station at 8 o'clock in the morning. In the strictest possible terms, the Foreign Office forbids you or me telling anyone else about this. Do you understand this, John?"

Dad remained unmoved, staring at Principal Chance.

I felt a strange mixture of elation and fear. Elated that
Mair had asked for me specifically and fearful that I was
being caught up in the machinery of government. It was
most peculiar and of course I agreed to everything that the
Principal requested of me.

As I was about to leave his book lined study, the Principal
leant into me as though someone might be listening and said,
"John fach, I don't know what your friend is up to but she
must be very important." I smiled and realised that I had no
idea what it was she was doing for the Foreign Office.

The following day John arrived at the railway station at the appointed
time. At the booking office he received an envelope containing a
train ticket and some cash for expenses. An anonymous note was
also included, telling him to take a taxi from the railway station to
which he was headed and ask for the Foreign Office.

I was to wait until Miss Thomas was brought out to meet me.
This was no ordinary ticket but for the first and only time
in my life, we would be travelling first class. As I took my seat
in the first class compartment I felt strangely out of place;
around me were army officers and some business people deep
in newspapers. But I was excited to be on such a strange
and mysterious assignment. As I looked out at the passing
landscape, there were signs of devastation everywhere; Bristol,
Swindon, Oxford all bore the marks of the Blitz. When we
arrived in Bletchley station, it seemed such an anti-climax.
Compared to London this was a village; hard to believe that
the Foreign Office would have any interest in the place.

The note was true to itself. I was taken by taxi to a gate
which led apparently to a country house commandeered by

the Foreign Office. I wasn't allowed to go in and eventually Mair came out looking pale and thin. She was so happy to see me but as soon as we got on the train she fell soundly asleep and didn't wake until we got back to Cardiff.

I found out that her flu and exhaustion was largely influenced by her appalling landlords. The husband's behaviour seemed to amount to mental cruelty, threatening to listen out for any secrets Mair might blurt out in her sleep. The poor thing was so overwrought by his threats and overworked in her work that her health finally collapsed.

We drew very close during that period. Mair was of course interested in the IVF and gladdened to hear that all was going well. It was noticeable that we started referring to a future together, not directly in terms of marriage but it was evident that we could conceive of life after the war that contained each other. Mair was under considerable strain and I could tell she wanted to talk about BP as she called it. I didn't press the matter but after a week or so she shared a few things with me that I probably shouldn't have known about. It was clear that she needed to talk about her experiences, and even though she couldn't tell me much, I learnt that Mair was involved in decrypting German codes. It was, she said, impossible work.

Mair returned home again for the Christmas holidays and John had decided that he must act swiftly. After paying a visit to Mair's father in Pontycymer and receiving a favourable reply, he visited a pawnshop in the city centre. The combination of family support, preaching, and his ARP salary had enabled him to save a small amount of money, enough to buy a ring.

I didn't recall seeing any jeweller's shops in the centre; maybe they were there and I hadn't noticed. But there were any number of pawn shops around and I'd heard that this was the best place to buy engagement rings. I knew that this would be a stop gap until we could afford something more expensive after the war but I wanted to have a ring in my possession for the moment when I would ask the question of her.

Without knowing her finger size or indeed her jewel preferences, John left the shop with the ring tucked away in a small box. This was where it was kept whilst John had a few days with his family in Gorseinon and Mair spent the holidays in Pontycymer. Eventually they reunited in Swansea on New Year's Day 1942, where the young couple had arranged to spend the day together.

I met Mair in Swansea station and we took the tram to the Mumbles. I was very nervous and a little quiet. Now the day had arrived I wasn't sure how to broach the subject without it seeming very forced and unnatural. On the other hand I knew the subject of marriage wouldn't rise naturally. Mair however was very garrulous and rather exercised by the Christmas she'd endured. Her formidable aunts had spent time at her father's house and somehow or another an almighty row had erupted. It sounded as though they had ganged up on her. It seemed that her decision to leave for Mount Hermon after her mother died was still an issue of contention. They thought then and still did, apparently, that her place was at home looking after her father. They weren't supportive of her years at university and simply refused to believe that she was now working for the Foreign Office. They more or less accused her of lying. At some point Mair lost her temper and displayed her fury. She is a steely and determined character and not one to take that sort of accusation lightly. Well she let them have it by the sounds of things, and when we met in Swansea she needed to talk it through.

After lunch we went for a walk on the beach with the whole beauty of Swansea Bay curving around. I could feel time ebbing away and without knowing what else to do I dropped to my knees in front of Mair. I fumbled for the box in my jacket pocket and somehow through my nerves I asked her for her hand in marriage. I knew she was the girl for me and I was utterly convinced that God had brought us together and even though we had only known each other for just over a year I couldn't have been more sure of anything. I loved her strength of mind and spirit; in short I knew that I loved her. But in that moment as I knelt, I had no idea how she might respond. Mercifully she gave an unhesitating yes and as we embraced we prayed together. It was a moment of great tenderness and joy.

CHAPTER 14

Let Me Now Be God's Soldier

As already mentioned, my father loved books, especially those of the theological variety and his children's shelves are now crammed with them, many tatty and fading. Like our parents, my siblings and I are hoarders. A number of these books date from the war period; and one of them has a long title: *A letter to Great Britain from Switzerland*. Published in 1941, its author was Karl Barth, famous for his commentary on Romans and the Barmen Declaration. Barth and the German Confessing Church had been fearless in condemning the idolatry of the Nazi cause, but in this book, Barth backed Churchill's determination to use military might against Germany. This was a just war and Britain and her allies must not capitulate to German aggression. To turn a blind eye to the Third Reich and allow the innocents to suffer would be worse than using force to disarm Hitler and his supporters.

There's another book next to that one, written by a less famous academic. In fact his reputation has not survived. Authored by G. H. C. Macgregor D.D. D.Litt, its title is *The New Testament Basis of Pacifism* and here's an extract underlined by my dad:

But he who is committed to the Christian Pacifist faith
quickly discovers that he is committed to more than perhaps
he at first realized. As one eminent prominent Pacifist
has admirably put it: "There is something shockingly
inconsistent in the man who grows indignant about
international war, yet is content to grow rich out of the
present industrial system, to see its disputes settled by force,
open or disguised, and generally to live by a scale of values
which is entirely acquiescent in its tangled and ruptured
personal relationships."[1]

Professor Macgregor is arguing for pacifism as a subset of
international socialism, not a position adopted by many Christians at
the time. As far as I can see, many of the well-known Christian writers
during World War Two backed the just war theory. As a theologian,
serious about his faith, my father must have been familiar with this
line of thought but I have no memory of him talking about it. This
theory is the way many Christians understood the necessity for
Britain's declaration of war against Germany, a view articulated by C.
S. Lewis, another one of my dad's favourite authors. In a letter to the
editor of the journal *Theology* in 1939, Lewis defended the just war
theory by way of analogy about a hangman. Before the executioner
performs his death duty, the guilty person has previously been
found guilty under the due process of law. Providing the hangman
is satisfied that the judicial system is fair, then he has a duty to carry
out his responsibilities. If it transpires that he hangs an innocent
person then a sin has been committed but not by him.

I submit that the rules for determining what wars are
just were originally rules for the guidance of princes, not
subjects. This does not mean that private persons must

obey governments commanding them to do what they know is sin but perhaps it does mean (I write it with some reluctance) that the ultimate decision as to what the situation at a given moment is in the highly complex field of international affairs is one which must be delegated.

In a lecture given to a pacifist society in 1941 (subsequently published as *Why I Am Not a Pacifist*), Lewis argued that pacifism is wrong on the basis of facts, intuition, reasoning, and authority, and accused pacifists of being "entirely mistaken". Far from creating a better world, it allowed tyrants to do as they pleased without defending the needs and safety of others.

My father would have understood the argument but he would not have sympathized with it. The responsibility for taking the life of another lay with the individual and could not be delegated to the state. He would probably have accused its proponents of using the Bible for ideological purposes: making the state and themselves feel better about the most pointless human activity of all. As far as he was concerned, the teaching of Jesus was unequivocal – killing another person was always wrong and could not be justified in any circumstance.

But I can also see a look of mischief break over his sightless face and with it the accusation that the established churches were always toadying up to the powers that be. I suspect he believed that the just war theory was simply a fancy way of allowing governments to get away with murder. Real Christianity was radical and didn't look good in cassocks and stoles. Moreover any church that needed royal patronage wasn't worth the embossed letterhead it was printed on.

Like many other issues, whether or not Christians should fight in times of war has been a polarizing issue in the church for centuries.

During World War One, the position adopted by the churches and chapels was ambivalent. Alongside movements which campaigned for the rights of conscientious objectors, some clergy actively encouraged men to sign up for service as part of their Christian duty. Once war had been declared on Germany, Chancellor of the Exchequer David Lloyd George encouraged the establishment of a Welsh Army. This duly happened and Lloyd George appointed John Williams, a Calvinistic Methodist minister from Brynsiencyn, Anglesey, as its chaplain general and chief recruiter and gave him the rank of colonel. Williams travelled extensively through Welsh-speaking communities championing the war and using the pulpit to attract more recruits. Wearing military uniform and his ministerial collar, he gained a reputation as one of the war's most efficient recruiting sergeants. By 1915, 100,000 Welshmen had joined the forces, the number rising to 270,000 by 1918. However, 35,000 of these men did not return, making one of the highest per capita losses of any of the nations involved in the war.

When conscription finally came into force in 1916, the Military Service Act also recognized the work of numerous peace organizations which had lobbied for a conscientious objection clause. In total, around 16,000 COs were registered. When the National Service (Armed Forces) Act came into force on 3 September 1939, as we have seen, the CO exemption was again recognized. The process for exemption was more or less identical to the one adopted in 1916. Like everyone else, COs had to enlist on the national register, declare their objection to war on grounds of conscience, and appear before a special tribunal to make their case and have their application judged. Tribunals could order full exemption, make it conditional on alternative service, grant exemption only from combatant duties, or dismiss the application completely.

Many COs, although not all of them, objected to war on the basis of religious convictions. This was certainly true of my father and many others whose dissent arose from centuries of Christian thought and practice. It was a culture that offered spiritual navigation around the Christian's obligation to the state. Whilst it was generally accepted that Christians, like everyone else, should render unto Caesar that which is Caesar's, there were exceptions. Going to war was one of them. It was a point of view that tried to balance the need for authentic obedience to Jesus Christ whilst at the same time advocating the need for good citizenship and participation in civic society.

This tradition of dissent started early in the history of the church and then threaded its way through the following centuries. Writing towards the middle of the second century AD, Justin Martyr said:

> We who were filled with war, and mutual slaughter and
> every wickedness… have changed our warlike weapons
> – our swords into ploughshares, and our spears into
> implements of tillage – and we cultivate piety, righteousness,
> philanthropy, faith, and hope, which we have from the
> Father Himself through Him who was crucified.[2]

Another major theologian, Origen, writing in AD 248, recognized that Christians must serve their natural rulers, but through prayer and not military service:

> And we do take our part in public affairs, when along
> with righteous prayers we join self-denying exercises
> and meditations, which teach us to despise pleasures,
> and not to be led away by them. And none fight better

for the king than we do. We do not indeed fight under
him, although he require it; but we fight on his behalf,
forming a special army – an army of piety – by offering
our prayers to God.[3]

Martin of Tours (316–97) became a Christian after a career as a
soldier and when ordered to fight for the Roman empire in the
Gallic provinces (now Germany), he is alleged to have said to the
emperor Julian:

Until now I have served you as a soldier. Let me now be
God's soldier, I am a soldier for Christ. It is no longer
lawful for me to fight.[4]

However, a game-changing moment came in the fifth century with
St Augustine's attempt to define what he termed a just war. Writing
at a period when the Roman empire was breaking down under
attack from barbarian armies, Augustine's views represented a shift
from the two earlier viewpoints. Christians, he said, belonged to
two kingdoms: that of heaven and that of the world, with duties
to accept the authority of both realms. As exemplary citizens, they
must obey the civil authorities. So how should Christians respond
to the emperor's decree? In his work *City of God*, Augustine said
there are four conditions needed for a just war, and Christians
should weigh these carefully before enlisting in the military:

- **Just authority**: has there been a legitimate legal and political
  process in support of this war?
- **Just cause**: is the degree of the wrong caused sufficient to
  merit going to war?
- **Right intention**: is this response proportionate to the wrong it
  addresses?

- **Last resort**: have all other means been exhausted?

When the state entered into a war which Augustine deemed to be morally just, then it was the Christian's duty to take up arms with a clean conscience.

At the time of the Reformation, neither Luther nor Calvin was a pacifist. Luther adopted Augustine's two kingdoms hypothesis: the Christian was under an obligation to obey both rulers and had no right to be selective. Calvin saw the state as being God's servant and in times of war the Christian had a duty to bear arms. In Calvin's terminology, the magistrate was both a servant of God and a civic ruler. In administering the laws of God and directing the affairs of the city, he was to be obeyed.

During the English Civil War (1642–49) an important doctrinal document was published that had a profound impact on the Church of England and continues to form the theological basis of Presbyterian denominations worldwide as well as a number of other Protestant denominations. In order to forge a closer allegiance with the anti-monarchist parties in Scotland, and at the insistence of the Church of Scotland, the English Parliament convened a gathering of 121 senior Puritan clergymen in Westminster to reform the Church of England according to the standards and practices already in force in Scotland. There, the entire ecclesiastical apparatus had been changed. Episcopalian bishops no longer led the church; instead local elders (presbyters) were in charge, while Calvin's theology was taught in all the churches. The resulting document produced by this meeting in 1646 was called the Westminster Confession of Faith and, among other matters, it defined the Christian's duty to obey the civil powers when war with another state is deemed to be just:

It is lawful for Christians to accept and execute the office of a magistrate when called thereunto; in the managing whereof, as they ought especially to maintain piety, justice, and peace, according to the wholesome laws of each commonwealth, so, for that end, they may lawfully, now under the New Testament, wage war upon just and necessary occasion.

(Westminster Confession 23.2)

But my father's cultural influences stemmed more from the so-called radical reformation, which had taken Luther's teaching that Christians should read the Bible for themselves, and come up with ideas he had never expected. Luther and others drew a distinction between the visible and invisible church; only God could judge true believers from everyone else and so church and state were intertwined. Radical reformers such as the Anabaptists took a different line. The church consisted of believers only, evidenced through the believer's baptism, and their allegiance was to God and not the state. There was a total separation between church and state, and the Christian's duty was always to obey God's law rather than the king's. Menno Simons, an Anabaptist and founder of the Mennonites, argued that all Scripture should be interpreted through the lens of Christ. Thus when dealing with Old Testament passages which glorified warfare, he said: "All Scripture is interpreted according to the spirit, teaching, walk and example of Christ and the apostles."[5] An early recognition of conscientious objection was granted to the Dutch Mennonites in 1575. They could refuse military service in exchange for a monetary payment.

The Anabaptist view on pacifism was articulated centuries later in a statement made at a conference in Kansas on 2 November 1935:

War is sin. It is the complete denial of the Spirit, Christian love and all that Christ stands for. It is wrong in spirit and method, and destructive in results. Therefore we cannot support or engage in any war, or conflict between nations, classes or groups.[6]

This Anabaptist rejection of warfare strongly influenced the Baptist denominations of Great Britain. Through faith and baptism, Christians were now under the rule of another king and citizens of his kingdom. Whilst under a general duty to obey worldly rulers and governments, this only extended to laws which conformed to the Bible as they understood it. In situations when Christians were expected to break Christ's law, such as conscription, the individual believer had a right to exercise their conscience and say no. And they weren't alone, joined as they were by Quakers and some members of other Christian groups, most notably Plymouth Brethren, Pentecostals, Salvationists (Salvation Army), Methodists, Jehovah's Witnesses, and Christadelphians.

The most significant pacifist voice in the UK however came from the Society of Friends (Quakers), founded by George Fox during the English Civil War in the seventeenth century. Like other continental groups, the Quakers refused to bear arms on the grounds of conscience. Their successful resistance led to the Militia Ballot Act of 1757, specifically allowing Quakers exemption from military service.

The most well-known statement of this belief was given in a declaration to King Charles II of England in 1660 by George Fox and eleven others:

All bloody principles and practices we do utterly deny, with all outward wars, and strife, and fightings with outward weapons, for any end, or under any pretence whatsoever, and this is our testimony to the whole world. That spirit of Christ by which we are guided is not changeable, so as once to command us from a thing as evil and again to move unto it; and we do certainly know, and so testify to the world, that the spirit of Christ, which leads us into all Truth, will never move us to fight and war against any man with outward weapons, neither for the kingdom of Christ, nor for the kingdoms of this world.[7]

Other Christian pacifist streams before, during, and after the two world wars, came from ecumenical organizations, including the Fellowship of Reconciliation (FOR), a Christian pacifist organization. The FOR arose in 1914 out of a friendship forged between a German Lutheran and an English Quaker, when Friedrich Siegmund-Schultz and Henry Theodore Hodgkin met at an ecumenical conference in Switzerland. Before leaving and on the eve of war, they pledged to do all they could to work towards peace, even in times of conflict. Siegmund-Schultz is reported to have said to Hodgkin: "Whatever happens, nothing is changed between us. We are one in Christ and can never be at war."

Hodgkin returned to Britain and the remainder of his 1914 was spent campaigning for the rights of men who refused to bear arms on religious and moral grounds. The FOR was founded in December that year at a conference in Cambridge. The conference made a series of five declarations based on the incompatibility of war with the love of God. The third declaration gave the basis of conscientious objection:

That therefore, as Christians, we are forbidden to wage war, and that our loyalty to our country, to humanity, to the

Church Universal, and to Jesus Christ our Lord and Master, calls us instead to a life-service for the enthronement of Love in personal, commercial and national life.[8]

Critics accused them of liberal naivety. The FOR was built on an assumption that if enough people of goodwill joined together and sought peace then they would succeed. Others criticized the FOR and later peace movements for championing an optimistic and evolutionary approach to history. They were accused of defining the kingdom of God according to Western civilization's technological, scientific, and educational innovations, and thinking that better healthcare, literacy, and knowledge would cure the world of its ills. My father may have been many things, but naive he was not. If anything he could be unerringly pessimistic about the human race. The man whose preaching I remember railed against sin. It was for him the essential flaw in every person, the snag that wrecked every human enterprise. This would lead him to explain the purpose of Christ's redeeming death, but the insinuating clutch of sin was never far away. This tendency could leave a somewhat negative perception amongst his congregations. I remember a middle-aged member of one of his churches remarking that whenever she listened to my father she invariably felt depressed about the state of her life. My cousin Gareth Morris remembers a conversation he had with a deacon of my father's church in Llanelli. He said, "He was the most miserable minister Seion ever had."

This is unfair; my dad's preaching was thoughtful, serious about communicating the Bible, compassionate, and Christ-centred. He was also a man of sparkling wit and good company. But I also understand the sentiment. He was a depressive by nature – not I think in a clinical sense, but by dint of oversensitivity and a tendency to withdraw into himself. It didn't help his mental cause that he became identified with church networks and groupings that managed to eclipse the glory of God's love with the minor moon of sectarianism.

CHAPTER 15

1943, a Badly Chewed Suit

I'm looking at a blue hardback book with a blue and yellow dust jacket, entitled *Christianity and Some Living Religions of the East* by Sydney Cave D.D., published in London in 1929. It has 218 pages and is priced at four shillings.

On the inside cover is someone's name and a date, crossed out:

~~Dorothy Finch~~
~~April 1943~~

And underneath it reads:

T.R. Jones.
A reminder of Shoreditch

This book was a gift to my dad after a summer placement at a church in Shoreditch. His three-month residency in the East End left a lasting impression on him, with its dense and multicultural population. London was unlike anywhere he had lived before and he found it enchanting. He never mentioned Dorothy Finch as part of his reminiscences, but she, presumably, was the volume's previous owner. She clearly thought that it would be helpful to Dad, a spur to study the relationship between Christianity and other religions. And this was one of the challenges he must have faced: presenting Christ among the Jews, Muslims, Hindus, and Sikhs of Shoreditch. Published between the two world wars, this is how the book's author summed up the challenge in the final chapter:

> If we offer Christianity to the East as the religion of the
> West, we shall offer it in vain. It is to be preached, not as the
> religion of the West, but as a religion for the world, whose
> full meaning will not be realised until its universality ceases
> to be a mere postulate of faith, and becomes an achievement
> of service.[1]

In the summer of 1942, John accepted a three-month placement in the Shoreditch Tabernacle, a large Baptist church in the East End of London. The church boasted a regular Sunday congregation running into several hundred with its own children's congregation led by and for children. His trip to the city with Mair had whetted his appetite for more and he was eager to experience the diverse culture of the capital city. Its proximity to Bletchley gave him hope that he would see more of Mair than he might otherwise.

*I arrived on an unusually warm day in July and when
I came out of the underground station in Shoreditch I
was immediately struck by aromas I'd never smelt before.
Spices, oils, fried fish and meat all mingling together. And
skin colours that were novel to me. I don't think I'd seen a
black face growing up in Gorseinon, and in Cardiff the only
African or West Indian people I'd met all lived in the area
of the docks. And the only times I saw them were on the few*

occasions I went with the SCM to hand out food in that area.
But this was different. There were fewer white faces and a far
greater representation from people from all over the world.
I was so overwhelmed by this initial experience, I stood still
and watched. This was a place of business and industry: fruit
sellers, greengrocers, cafés and restaurants, street markets,
barbers of all descriptions. It felt like a different planet to
Wales.

I'd heard people talk about London smog but until I'd
lived there I couldn't have imagined what it was like. I was
familiar with the soot and poor air quality of the valleys but
London was on a scale of its own. Wherever you walked
there were factories and tall chimneys belching black air into
the sky. And there were any number of tailors and sewing
shops. There was industry everywhere and people living on
top of each other. Most days there were street vendors selling
freshly baked bagels, a kind of bread favoured by the Jews,
and of course any number of fish and chip shops and even
people selling ice cream on the street.

He was working under the supervision of the church's minister, a
man in his fifties. John was blown away by the large congregations
who gathered in the church every Sunday:

The minister lived out in Harrow and travelled by rail to
Shoreditch every day. He was smartly dressed in pinstripes
and a bowler hat. He told me that he wore a wing collar and
silk tie as far as central London, where he would change into
a dog collar. Mind you when it came to tobacco, he was less
secretive; he was always puffing on a cigar.

John was given accommodation with a young couple who lived in a large house near the church on Hackney Road. He was housed in the attic room, a large, dusty, unused space in the roof of the house. And he soon realized he had company.

I had a sturdy but uncomfortable bed which squeaked every time I moved. Eventually I got used to it, but it was so noisy to begin with that I was constantly waking up in the night. I would lie there trying to sleep, listening to this persistent scratching noise. I knew that sound, it was the sound of mice scurrying. I'd seen plenty of these in my early days in Loughor Common so I wasn't greatly disturbed, particularly as I imagined they were probably running behind the skirting boards.

Within a few weeks, however, the full impact of the rodents' presence was seen by all:

After I'd been in the "Tab", as people called it, for a short while, I was asked to lead a Sunday morning service. This was a huge honour as I knew the church had a fine preaching history, and there would be a large congregation. This would necessitate the wearing of my best suit, given to me by Mam and Dat when I started in Cardiff. I felt sure that a crisp white shirt with a starched collar and smart grey suit would help cover my nervousness. Sunday arrived and after more sermon preparation and prayer, I opened the wardrobe and took out the suit and shirt hanging together. The shirt was neatly creased and fitted me well. As I slipped into the trousers I could feel that something wasn't quite right but maybe it just needed the jacket to make the experience more

*familiar. The jacket however didn't fit as well as it normally
did. Closer examination revealed the truth. The mice had
gnawed and chewed the lining, right through in some
places, reducing my Sunday best to rags. My landlords were
mortified by my predicament and assured me that measures
would be taken to get rid of the mice. In the meantime they
felt sure that the landlord's best suit would make a good
substitute for the pulpit. It was a lovely gesture but given that
he was a little shorter than me and considerably more portly,
my debut that Sunday morning must have seemed comical
to the gathered congregation. I was constantly hitching the
trousers up and tucking my shirt in!*

The publication of a book in 1983 jogged John's East End war
memories:

Looking at the History of Christianity *today, I noticed that
its chief editor is Dr Tim Dowley and I wondered if that
were the son of Roger and Ruth Dowley. During the summer
vacation in the war I stayed at their home in the East End
of London and from them – not so much what they said but
what they were – I learned a great deal about the radical and
far reaching implications of the faith.*

During his three months in London, John and Mair were able
to spend some time with each other and John visited Speakers'
Corner in Hyde Park on several occasions:

*I was eager to hear Donald Soper speak as I'd heard so
much about him. He was the leading Christian advocate
for resistance to war and was completely unashamed in his*

views. He was a small, avuncular sort of man, even back then. Well spoken and humorous, he always spoke his mind but was always respectful to his audience. His talks were always Christ-centred; Soper started with Jesus and ended with him. He would sometimes refer to something in the news, or quote a piece of poetry, but more than anything else he wanted his hearers to know that he was speaking on behalf of his Lord. He would generally give each address a title such as: Why Jesus is against war; why the poor are paying for the rich man's folly; the kingdom of God is within you; the cross and the bomb are never friends. And he drew enormous crowds; I remember him saying once that he wanted the largest church in the city and to do that he needed to get beyond the four walls.

On one occasion the crowd stood about ten rows deep; there must have been close to a thousand people listening to him. Generally people listened well; there were always hecklers but that was part of the experience. Soper's retorts were always choice; at times funny or direct, but never rude. There were a few times however when things turned a little ugly. I saw him getting jostled, objects being thrown and some very hostile words shouted at him. But he was unflappable and somehow brought everything back to Jesus' way of love. Time after time I heard the same accusation levelled at pacifists, that we should be ashamed of ourselves, of our cowardice and willingness to let others suffer in our place. I wanted to tell people that ours was a different kind of bravery. Refusing to go along with the tide of public opinion and obeying the still small voice of conscience has always struck me as a more honourable course of action, requiring a great deal more courage than simply accepting the received wisdom of the day.

But I also realised that his theology was no longer mine. Whilst I deeply admired his focus on Christ and his passion for building God's Kingdom on earth, I felt that there was a naivety to his approach. It seemed to me back then, and still does, that unless the horror of the human condition is resolved, all our good endeavours aren't worth a thing. Jesus came to rescue us from our plight not through declaring a better manifesto than anyone else but by dying in our place and transforming our hearts.

Yet again John found himself in an isolated space. He'd thrown his lot in with a school of thought that emphasized the differences between the church and the world. To be a Christian meant rescuing people from the clutches of the world, the flesh, and the devil. By now, Dad's pacifism had become largely an expression of his private piety, detached from the wider vision of other Conchies. He was on his own. And he – and his family – had discovered that most people had little regard for Conchies:

In general most people were unsympathetic towards men who refused to fight. Even in the Baptist college there was no consensus that following your conscience was an honourable thing. A few men had signed up as chaplains and apparently some of the new intake had deferred their places until after the war. But by and large most of the men and faculty understood the position I and one or two others had taken. The same applied in the university; if anything the atmosphere was militantly anti-war. I came across a number with strong socialist, even communist tendencies, who saw the war as another attack on the workers by aggressive capitalism.

I encountered more of a reaction as an ARP warden.
Most of the other wardens were older men who couldn't fight
and so the younger wardens stood out. My fellow wardens
were mostly genially indifferent to the reasons why I hadn't
been conscripted. They probably knew I was training to
be a minister and thought no more of it. I did have a few
lengthier discussions with some of my colleagues on quieter
shifts. One of them told me he had fought in the First World
War and had lost a number of friends. He told me I should
be ashamed of myself for not supporting the nation in its
hour of crisis. He opined that the country needed more
soldiers and fewer vicars. But by and large I escaped largely
unscathed as an ARP warden. I got used to being called a
Conchie by the public, and a few times I overheard some of
the women bemoaning the fact while their husbands were
fighting abroad, here was I wearing a tin hat in the safety of
Cardiff.

But John remembered a man he met later in his life who had also
registered as a conscientious objector and experienced extreme
reactions:

He was a Pentecostal from the north of England, not a pastor
but an ordinary church member. When Neville Chamberlain
took the country into war, he knew that he couldn't be a
soldier. He was about my age and had become a Christian in
his teens. More than anything else he said he wanted to serve
Jesus Christ and live a life that pleased him. He reasoned
that since the Ten Commandments forbade taking the life of
another human being and Jesus commanded his followers to
turn another cheek when assaulted by their enemies, he had

no choice. He registered as a CO and immediately faced the fury of his family and colleagues. His father had fought in the Great War and received medals for his bravery. On the day his son took this decision of conscience his father refused to speak to him again, such was the shame he felt. Similar treatment was meted out by his siblings, mother and wider family. They however kept the channels of communication open but the issue was a deep stain that could never be erased. His office colleagues also ostracised him. He worked in the county council and suffered a great deal of silent rejection.

But it was John's parents who bore the brunt of the criticism. They kept silent during the war, for fear of upsetting their only son.

Neither Mam nor Dat enjoyed good health; especially Mam. She feared ill health and often expressed this in terms of being destined to live a short life. She had known great hardship and poverty, especially when Dat was laid off work and I think this anxiety had taken its toll. She was very sensitive to harsh words but delighted in her home and family. When they learnt of my decision to register as a conscientious objector, they were fully supportive. I suspect they would have been happier if I'd not made a fuss and accepted my legal exemption as a minister. But they understood my reasoning and Dat in particular respected my views. From the time I told them in Christmas 1940, I barely went home to Gorseinon for any length of time. My ARP duties and other studies meant I didn't have a great deal of contact with them at all. Little did I know that Mam and Dat suffered some nasty criticism because of me.

*When I went before the tribunal in Cardiff, there were
a few journalists present, reporting on the events. Some
of these reports ended up in the local press, as one of the
reporters acted on behalf of a number of different titles.
Some of the tribunal hearings were sent to news agencies
and the* Manchester Guardian *carried regular reports from
tribunals, including Cardiff. I can only assume that the local
papers in Swansea must have carried the report from my
tribunal, because a number of people back home knew of my
decision. People whom we didn't know socially at all who
could only have found out by other means than the family.*

Mam was given an object used in the First World War to shame
men that had not gone to war. Before conscription in 1915,
Admiral Charles Fitzgerald founded the "Organisation of the
White Feather". Its purpose was to publicly shame young, able-
bodied men who hadn't enlisted in the army. As fewer and fewer
men volunteered to fight, so the organization grew more militant
in its practice of handing out white feathers. Women would walk
up to strangers, upbraid them for their cowardice, and give them
a feather. The leading pacifist of the age, Fenner Brockway, joked
that he had been given enough white feathers to make a fan. The
practice ended with conscription in 1916 but its vivid symbolic
imagery was remembered for decades later:

*I discovered that on more than one occasion Mam had been
given a white feather whilst out shopping. Generally this
was always accompanied by a patronising statement such as
"You poor woman. You must feel so ashamed of your son's
cowardice," or words to that effect. These feathers were given
by complete strangers, or rather they lived in the area but*

had no connection with my parents. This shook my mother badly and for a period she stayed at home and other people did the shopping for her. The woman grew fearful that people were talking about her behind her back. She was highly sensitive anyway and this sort of thing made matters worse.

But John was still a marked man. Whatever his inner changes, he had gone on public record as a conscientious objector and had to accept whatever was thrown at him in the court of public opinion. For this he was prepared, but he was shaken by another incident involving his parents:

We lived in a very close community in Brynhyfryd Road and we all knew each other's business. During the days of the great depression and the General Strike, everyone pulled together and made sure that people were cared for. That practice still existed but it was clear that the war placed a greater strain on these relationships. One couple in particular took great exception to my decision and made their feelings known. The worst occasion took place one Sunday when Mam and Dat arrived home from church on foot. As they turned into the front gate, the lady in question came from a nearby house and started railing at them. Her son was a soldier in the Army, serving his country with a clear conscience. How could they go to church and look so holy when they were just being hypocritical? They should tell John to do something worthwhile and serve his country and then get a proper job after the war. My father tried to intervene and stop the tirade but she wasn't having any of it. Whilst her son was laying his life down in some far away land, the likes of me were having a lovely holiday in Britain. I should be ashamed; they should be ashamed because the whole of Gorseinon certainly was. My parents were devastated by this experience and I'm not sure my mother really recovered from it. Her poor nerves were shot through by the end of the war, gnawed away by anxiety and fear.

When I heard these tales, I was mortified. My high principles and pure conscience had brought misery upon them. I'd barely tasted any real criticism and anyway I'd moved to a city where few people knew me, but they hadn't asked for this. Not only did I regret that this had happened to them, I regretted my decision in the first place. I adored my parents and I would have done anything for them. To avoid their pain I should have kept quiet about my conscientious objection and simply accepted the exemption afforded to me under the Act of Parliament.

I heard my father repeat this several times and he meant every word. Like his mother, my dad was deeply sensitive to the words and actions of others and he could not bear the pain and anguish he had caused them. Maybe this explains in part why he said so very little about his CO status during his college years. He was all too aware of the consequences of his actions and wanted to ameliorate this damage. Joining an organization, banging a drum, marching in a parade would draw attention to a decision which in the end was deeply personal to him.

That summer, John also visited Mair in BP. He had been there once before, as we have seen, to accompany her home during a period of illness in her first few months; but this time it was different. They were engaged to be married and fully committed to each other. His visit was memorable:

I remember sitting outside BP, fascinated at the people leaving and arriving. They were so different to either of us, very much of the Oxbridge set; confident, well-spoken and loud. And the clothing on display was peculiar. Many of the men wore baggy cricket jumpers, sometimes with a bow tie. Others however looked as though they were dressed in dinner suits, when in reality they were working in offices. And the women who worked there had a similarly avant-garde approach. All sorts of frocks and dresses, but the thing that struck me most was their stockings! They were multi-coloured, even garish. A few of them wore odd-coloured stockings. I couldn't imagine that this would be accepted in Cardiff; and in Gorseinon there would be uproar!

This episode raises all kinds of questions about my father, particularly about how much he knew of the work carried out in BP. Bearing in mind that the identity of its location was a matter of national security, this was now his second time there. Whilst he never entered BP itself, he understood that it existed to decipher German codes. This information on its own was probably in breach of the Official Secrets Act. Apart from Prime Minister Churchill and a handful of senior civil servants, no one seems to have known the nature of BP's work. The Axis powers fought the entire war with no knowledge of BP's success in routinely intercepting and deciphering their coded messages. How it all remained a secret remains one of the war's greatest mysteries, particularly as it employed over 10,000 people by 1945. But the secrecy was maintained by them and by my father.

His ability to maintain a confidence remained one of his strongest features. Whether it was the content of his pastoral encounters, or his own issues of conscience, he was silent.

Whatever the dilemmas, turmoil, contradictions of his position, he kept quiet. He would have made a good spy.

Maybe the most telling silence of all concerns the disagreement that must have existed between my father and mother on the issue of war. He was a pacifist and she essentially a member of the armed forces. My mother reconciled it this way: "My actions weren't directly harming or killing anyone and I think this helped us adapt to the differences between us."

But she also recognized that she was part of a team that enabled thousands of German planes, ships, and soldiers to be bombed. And she was painfully aware of occasions when British ships were allowed to be bombed by the enemy in case the cover of BP was blown.

They were married for sixty years and even though I remember them having differences of opinion and the occasional heated conversation, they never disagreed about the war. Or if they did, they conducted the argument away from the rest of the family or anyone else. And there was opportunity for them to disagree publicly. I recall a conversation over Sunday lunch in about 1974, when the subject of the war somehow made an appearance. I remember asking my mother about her role in the war and receiving her stock reply: "I worked for the Foreign Office in Bletchley Park."

And then my father launched his defence for pacifism and his anti-war stance. How military force was contrary to Christian principles, and politicians had forced people to betray their conscience. And it's significant that my mother said nothing. Significant because she wasn't that kind of person; she could be feisty, opinionated, and heated in debate. But on a subject of which she was an expert, even in generalities she chose to keep quiet.

So I wonder if this was part of their double act, because it happened a few times. Whenever the subject of war was raised, the same dynamic was rehearsed. As though they had somehow agreed that my father's outspokenness would take the heat from my mother and change the trajectory of the discussion.

CHAPTER 16

1944, a Love Letter to Piety

THE INTER-VARSITY FELLOWSHIP
OF EVANGELICAL UNIONS
39 BEDFORD SQUARE W.C.

Address to which reply should be sent:

Trinity College
Cambridge

1.3.44

Dear Russell

I have written to Glyn Owen about his becoming Welsh
Rep, though so far I have received no reply. If you see him
you might let him have details of the job etc. However
I am writing to ask if you will continue on the Exec for
another year. This would probably be as Vice Chairman…
I do hope you will feel that you can do this. As you know

the job entails practically nothing in the way of special duties, it is just the general Exec work really and I feel you will be able to manage that. I think in many ways it is clear that you are the man for the job and I do hope you will accept.

I am afraid I must not write more now. We are getting a bit behind with the nominations and want to get them out to the Unions soon, so I should be glad of a reply as soon as you feel clear about the Lord's will in the matter – if possible in a day or so. If you see Glyn I would be glad if you could ginger him up a bit too.

Excuse haste
Yours very sincerely
Oliver (Barclay)

Of the voluminous diaries, journals, exercise books, loose papers, and sermon notes scribbled on the backs of electricity bills and meeting agendas, this letter for me is the saddest. Whenever I read it I feel the suffocation of earnest evangelical zeal. It's a cheerfully busy note referencing its own corporate needs with no mention of the world outside. There are probably many reasons for this silence, not least that stories about the war were tightly controlled by the government. It's a hastily written business memo, so why should I expect it to have anything to say about the grind of war? It is unlikely that Oliver Barclay, the letter writer, could have known for example that in that same week the Germans had enslaved 5 million foreign nationals and forced them to work for the Third Reich. Or that more than 400 Italian civilians were asphyxiated on board a cargo train that stopped in a tunnel. But as I piece together my dad's writings at this time and compare them with others of the same persuasion, I'm finding a depressing consistency. A culture sealed within its own needs, with no ambition to address the horrors of the war. It reads to me like a love letter to pietism, an escape from the flames now covering much of Europe.

Like Dad, Oliver Barclay was a Conchie. A contemporary and fellow student with Barclay in Cambridge, Basil Atkinson, says this of him:

> He had come up in 1938 and was one of the few people
> in the country who obtained at the local tribunal absolute
> exemption from conscription, as a conscientious objector.
> I was present at the hearing of the tribunal and was able
> to note the respect paid by the chairman to his character
> and to his name, associated for so many generations with
> godliness.[1]

Dad received exemption whilst in his second year of a BD degree and his studies were spread across the university and the Baptist college, where the impact of the war was felt:

> A few students were called to the Forces, but only one lost
> his life, Hugh L Gittins who had volunteered for service
> with the RAF and who was lost over the English Channel.
> There was a steady flow of students passing through
> the College during the War years. Strange items soon
> appeared among the expenses: sand bags, stirrup pumps,
> ladders and payments to students for fire watching. Two
> students used to sleep in the building each night, on beds
> provided in the common room...[2]

In spite of the war and dwindling congregations, the vocation of church minister remained sought after. It has been estimated that for every two places in the denomination college in the pre World War Two years, there were over twenty applications. As we have seen, every candidate needed to have passed their Matriculation exams (roughly equivalent to today's A levels) and have a rudimentary understanding of New Testament Greek and Hebrew.

During the war years, a number of the ministerial students left the Baptist denomination to join either the Church in Wales or the Church of England. Among them was Selwyn Gummer, later a canon in the Church of England and father to John Selwyn Gummer (now Baron Deben), who served in Margaret Thatcher's government:

He was a pompous sort of man, but these were days of great uncertainty and change. A few years earlier it would have been harder to jump ship; you would have been seen as betraying a culture as much as anything. But the cultural climate was changing and I suppose in many ways this sort of thing was less noticeable and less interesting than it would have been earlier.

The culture and Christianity of the Baptist college were different to the more genteel and Anglican atmosphere of the IVF:

To a man, and we were all men apart from the Principal's wife, our politics was either socialist or liberal; there was a radical edge to our discussions. This radicalism spilt over into theology for quite a few of my friends, embracing the so called "new scholarship" coming in from Germany, much of which questioned the authenticity of the Bible and also traditional Christian doctrine. Even though he died in 1930, Adolf Von Harnack's influence was still keenly felt and taught. He reasoned that the New Testament had been largely influenced by later Greek patterns of thought and sought to identify what he deemed to be the authentic message of Jesus. He rejected the gospel of John, the Apostles' creed and questioned the credibility of the reported healings and miracles. Theologians such as Rudolf Bultmann also were peeling away the layers on the ancient texts of the gospels and discovering that Jesus the man was not the Messiah invented by the early church.

The college's influence on me was minimal in many ways. I greatly appreciated the community and love I found there as well as preaching class, but the main arena for me was the university. And when I began my theological studies in earnest from 1942 onwards, I really felt the clash between my academic studies and the influence coming my way through the IVF.

Two of his tutors were well recognized nationally and internationally. Theodore H. Robinson (1881–1964) was Professor of Semitic Languages and Aubrey Johnson, a gifted lecturer, was already marked for academic greatness. Robinson's reputation had put the new university on the scholastic map and through him and the staff he appointed, the department had gained a name for excellence.

He was a tall, imperious figure and had the air of a military general. He could seem distant and forbidding to begin with but he could be kindness itself to those in need. A number of students confided in him during periods of anxiety or distress and found him to be a real pastor to them.

Aubrey Johnson in particular made an impact on John. Although older than him, they had some similarities. Both men had known poverty and misfortune, and both went to Trefeca in order to qualify for university entry. Johnson's academic career was further punctuated by the sudden death of his mother, meaning he had to look after an older brother before taking his place in university. By the time John came to Cardiff, Johnson had acquired degrees from the universities of both Oxford and Halle-Wittenberg, as well as Cardiff. His lectures were inspiring, although his theology was markedly different to John's:

My tutorials with Prof Johnson were often lively. I had what is sometimes described as a "high" view of the Bible. I believed it was the word of God and contained all that was necessary for faith and practice. The professor, indeed the whole faculty, took a different view. Faith was essentially a subjective matter not grounded in the historicity or truth of the Bible. In fact the Bible was the product of literary sources from different eras in Israel's history and each source had its own emphasis and tradition. As far as the New Testament was concerned, Bultmann's view that the gospels had all been written a considerable time after the death of Jesus and had little historical value was vigorously championed.

My own studies led me to a very different conclusion to the ones being taught, and I frequently clashed with Professor Johnson. After one heated, but good-humoured exchange, he said to me, "John, when I'm on my knees in prayer I believe the same as you. I believe implicitly in the power of God to do as he wills but I cannot deny the evidence presented to me through academic study."

My dad never liked being labelled a conservative, not in theology or politics. This is how he expressed his feelings in 1983:

As far as the Evangelicals are concerned of course, there has been a pietistic refusal to relate the Gospel to social and political matters; its personalism has degenerated to an atomism that is frightening. And always there seemed to be the assumption that conservatism in theology means invariably conservatism in politics – an assumption that I find inexplicable and unwarrantable. The teachings of our Lord turned current accepted opinions on their head and surely, if they are believed, they cannot be reconciled with a complacent acceptance of the status quo. That is not to say that "Christ was the first socialist" or anything like that, but it is to say that "having the mind of Christ" involves his followers in seeing with his eyes, feeling with his heart and bringing to every issue all the energy of a renewed life.

It's hard reconciling my father's various contradictions. He was as angered by efforts to reduce the authority of the Bible as he was by attempts to rid the Bible of its socially radical message. My brother Iwan suggests that this dialectical tension could be seen in his pastoral care:

When he was visiting an individual or a family, his main concern was their well-being. I don't think it mattered to him whether they were gay or straight at that point; as a pastor he wanted to reach out to them in such a way that they felt valued and attended. I remember once being quite shocked at something he said to me. I had reported to him a conversation in which I had been involved on sexual ethics. At one point, the people I was debating with expressed an opinion that abortion was always wrong, whatever the circumstance. There could be no mitigating reason for allowing it whatsoever. When I told this to Dad, expecting him to agree with this position, he went very silent and then suggested that these issues were always complicated. He advised me to try and put myself in the shoes of a young woman who's been raped or a father who learns of his daughter's untimely pregnancy, before offering an opinion on the matter.

Again, in his 1983 diary, this is my father wrestling with his convictions:

Ethics for many evangelical Christians, if not confined to purely sexual morality, is individualistic and nothing to do with matters like social justice or international relations or war. It deals exclusively with one's daily walk and conduct before God and is not concerned overtly with the behaviour of people to each other in community and state or with international affairs. Any pre-occupation with matters of this nature is summarily dismissed as the "social gospel" and a denial of the pure New Testament Faith. It was not so that "I learned Christ"; my father was a devout Christian and at the same time an ardent trade unionist (who greatly bemoaned the excesses that even before his retirement were beginning to manifest themselves) and socialist. When I first went to the university, to be sure, there was a period of near pietism and quietism, but that could not be sustained indefinitely. And my reading of the Old Testament Prophets, together with the teaching of Jesus and his apostles, showed how untenable this narrowing of ethics is. Reading again in Amos today, I was reminded that God's concern is with the whole world – it isn't just social relationships within the nation of Israel that bring forth his denunciations but the inhumanity of the pagan nations round about. Here is ethical teaching in its wholeness which deserves the most reverent and profound study.

In the latter part of the war and after, the writing and example of the German pastor and theologian Dietrich Bonhoeffer captivated him. Bonhoeffer was one of the founding members of the German Confessing Church, along with a number of others. He established a seminary in Finkenwalde in north Germany for the training of pastors, from where he also wrote numerous books and papers and supervised his students and young ordinands as they served this "illegal" church. Sometime in 1941 he joined the *Abwehr*, the German Secret Service, which provided a cover for some high-ranking military men who wanted to depose Hitler. His role was to solicit support among his international ecumenical contacts for these aims. However, in 1944 Bonhoeffer was arrested and imprisoned as an accessory in the failed plot to assassinate Hitler. In 1945, he was executed.

Bonhoeffer took complete responsibility for his actions. He was unhappy with taking another's life but clearly believed that doing nothing in this situation was morally worse. Through his membership of the Abwehr *he had the opportunity to align himself with the plot to kill Hitler even though he too was a conscientious objector. I respected him enormously for his stance.*

And there's a savage irony here. Neither Barth nor Bonhoeffer was a pacifist. But Dad admired Bonhoeffer not only for his creative approach to theology, but also for his part in the plot to kill the Führer. Bonhoeffer was a man acting not on the orders of a general or politician, but on the basis of conscience, willing to take the consequences of his actions. I think my father genuinely understood Bonhoeffer's moral dilemma and even agreed with his stance. His copy of *Letters and Papers from Prison* is well thumbed and falling apart.

CHAPTER 17

Today I Had a Long Discussion with a Young Lady About Pacifism and Christianity

Here I have a burgundy-coloured, lined notebook with a hard cover. Most of the pages contain notes; some of these are sermons, others take the form of observations, reports, reflections, and book reviews. The writing is legible throughout, and produced using a fountain pen. Inside the front cover is a list of academic books, authors, and prices:

H.M Marshall Challenge of NT Ethics 15/-
The Way of Life (C.J. Barker), Lutterworth 21/-
Riddle of NT (Hoskyns and Davey) Faber 8/6

On the outside cover is a list of names, presumably of fellow students:

A Discussion About Pacifism and Christianity

Howard Jones
Derek Jennings
Nest Evans
Beryl Williams
Ray Looker
Freda Barlowe

The first entry comes three days after John's twenty-sixth birthday:

August 8 1944

What a strange idea people have of the Gospel! And how very different are conceptions of it from the message of Christ!

Today I had a long discussion with a young lady about pacifism and Christianity. It was not my intention or my choice to be embroiled in a fruitless argument, but having inadvertently been drawn into giving my opinions on this matter I found that it was essential for me to show why I held them. Needless to say, my notions were unacceptable (to state the matter very lightly) and were combated with spirit and considerable feeling.

That anyone should disagree with me on such a controversial issue as this has long since ceased to shock me, but what did disturb me was the way in which my "adversary" in debate chopped and changed the Gospel to her own ends and to justify her own particular point of view...

Most of my father's observations are found in notebooks such as this, and there are many others like it in similarly battered cloth covers. The one I have chanced upon has a more personal style and content. Here he is commenting on a conversation he's had with someone. Bearing in mind that this was the summer, it's unlikely to have taken place on the university campus. The setting for this heated exchange was probably one of his summer placements. Ministerial students were generally placed in smaller churches over the summer months to give them pastoral experience. It is likely that in the summer of 1944, John was based in a small church serving a large council estate on the outskirts of Caerphilly. Anchored at the foot of the Rhymney Valley, Caerphilly's industrial growth had come through its identity as an important railway town and also the presence of nearby coal mines. His "adversary" was unnamed but she was presumably a church member. And to me, this gives an added twist to the encounter. This was not student banter but a proper adult disagreement. In the nearby Aber Valley was the mining valley of Senghenydd, infamous for the 1913 mining disaster where over 400 men lost their lives in an explosion. His contretemps was probably with a working-class, Labour-voting resident. In short, they would have shared many of the same values, except he was a pacifist and she was clearly not.

His handwriting at this stage of his life was legible and clear; it would later become more of a scrawl, much like mine. There was a clear and unambiguous reference to his pacifist views but no real development of an argument. No indication of how he had arrived at this position or even the nature of the debate described. This entry simply stated that this was his viewpoint, disparaging of others who took a different view. That's how he dealt with controversial issues on the whole. Not quite "I'm right and you're wrong" but certainly with an appeal to his greater wisdom or authority.

At the time of this diary extract, John had just turned twenty-six and was about to start his final year at the University of South

Wales and Monmouthshire in Cardiff. In a year's time, he hoped to graduate and become an ordained Baptist minister.

The war had now entered a crucial phase since D-Day on 6 June, when the Allied troops, under General Eisenhower, had crossed the Channel to the Normandy coast and invaded German-held France. A decisive corner had been turned as the British and Allied troops formed an offensive line against a retreating German army. Despite the jubilation surrounding those landings, the following weeks and months were amongst the bloodiest and most attritional of the war. On the same day as my father's entry, a girl named Anne Frank, her sister, and her parents, with a few others, were captured in an Amsterdam attic and deported to the Westerbork prison camp. A few weeks later they were sent to Auschwitz. Only Anne's father survived.

And John hadn't heard from Mair for two months. Unbeknown to John and the rest of the world, Bletchley Park was in complete communications shutdown. No letters came out and none went in. Since D-Day, Mair and her colleagues had been working around the clock, breaking the intercepted Enigma codes and those of the other Axis powers. Her health was deteriorating, due largely to endless shifts and poor office ventilation. The amount of intercepted intelligence making its way to BP was staggering. By now the number of staff working at this top-secret establishment numbered over 10,000. It is mind-boggling considering it all began with a few dozen academics and civil servants in 1939.

The twenty-four-hour shift system was buckling under the pressure of keeping ahead of the Germans, so Mair and her colleagues just kept going day and night. Of Mair and the rest of the war effort, John was silent in this diary. His only interest was in reporting his feelings and spiritual development. Even this outburst about pacifism simply allowed him to sermonize about the woman's lack of spiritual depth. And this trend continued in the next entry:

August 25 1944

During this past week I have experienced a reawakened desire for reading and study; reawakened, I say, because it had for a period of weeks, even months, lain dormant. How true it is that sin not only enslaves the heart but also numbs the mind! This I have found out, with much pain and mental anguish during the recent past, and thus it is with joy that I find myself once again thirsting for knowledge – knowledge in its truest, deepest sense of consciousness of God and awareness of self. For all my reading has this one objective in view: to find in deeper measure the integration of soul and life that Christ alone is able to accomplish and the peace and harmony of soul that is bound to ensue.

With the Allies engaged in brutal combat with the Germans, the war was entering a vicious period. But this young man was consumed by the conflict raging within him:

… Sinful thoughts constantly battled against heavenly aspirations, my soul became the battle ground of the opposing forces of corruption and holiness, of the eternal and the temporal, spiritual and carnal and in the face of this ceaseless conflict, in which alas! the spiritual was too rarely victorious. The calm and rest of God gave way to a mood of what Pascal would call "desperation".

In his later years, he would eschew such pietism but here his writing showed little interest in the outside world. All that mattered to him was his war with the world, the flesh, and the devil. And I'm irritated and embarrassed. It's not as though these are isolated entries; this notebook is full of introspection. As tedious as these notes are, they contrast strongly with the 21-year-old who, five years earlier, went out of his way to be noticed for an act of public defiance. It's the same life and yet two different world views in a short period of time. Before the start of the autumn term, John attended an IVF leadership conference in High Leigh, Hertfordshire. It was a gathering of the executive committee and also the heads of the various IVF Christian unions. Keynote addresses were given by Martyn Lloyd Jones, Douglas Johnson, and John Stott. John returned to Cardiff deeply moved by the experience:

> *Perhaps the reaction that follows a time of blessing such as I experienced at the Leaders' Conference last week, is setting in. At any rate there has been a sort of restlessness in my soul today, a feeling of intense dissatisfaction with myself. This however is nothing new, and was inevitable after the searching addresses to which I listened at the Conference. What Christian or unbeliever could fail to be dissatisfied with his life on coming face to face with the Righteousness and the Glory of God?*

By the beginning of November, my father was disappearing down a rabbit hole of self-examination as he questioned himself:

> *Introspection is only of value therefore in telling us, by the help of God's Spirit, what is wrong; it serves to show us in our true colours and emphasises our desperate need and our*

terrible plight. It points us in the direction of our need for deliverance – and that must always lie beyond ourselves. We, bound as we are by our sinfulness, cannot break our own bonds, despite our longings that they should be thrown away. The Deliverer of the Captives is he who can break our fetters and make us free. It is the Holy Spirit of God indwelling us that enables us to have the victory!

And on it goes. I'm disturbed by my feelings of irritation; I don't want to feel like this. Like my father, I am a church minister and I have been keeping diaries and journals since I too was a student minister thirty years ago. As I read through those, too many of them are all about me and my inner monsters and torments. So why this reaction on my part, if I too am guilty of the same self-obsession? Furthermore, you could argue very convincingly that that's what keeping a diary or journal is all about. Christian spirituality is full of people who have kept journals and filled them with lament and verbal flagellation. Blaise Pascal, Madame Guion, John Bunyan, Jonathan Edwards, Robert Murray McCheyne, Samuel Rutherford, and many others have defined the genre, so why shouldn't this young man simply enjoy the genre of misery? I have and still do.

Here's my problem. This pristine new diary started with an account of a confrontation about pacifism and war; one that he didn't address. In fact his main concern was that she had deliberately misunderstood the Bible, whereas he had the correct interpretation.

Whether this verbal antagonist was a Christian or not, it is not my business to judge, but certain it is that she is expressive of many professing Christians in these days. What

pleases us in the New Testament, we accept, but anything
that does not fit into our little scheme of things we throw
overboard and reject. Where then is our Protestant belief
that the Holy Spirit shall illumine the inspired Word and
guide us into the realms of truth? This bastion of our faith
is fallen and the Scriptures are made subordinate to human
conceptions, sentiment and soulless rationalism.

Beyond this opening salvo, he withdrew deep into matters of the heart. But my father did have a story of dissent, his own strange war, and I'm hungry for the clues that lie beneath the surface. Five years earlier he had gone out of his way to be known as a Conchie, reduced now to an opaque conversation after a Sunday sermon. In the intervening years he hadn't joined any pacifist organizations, of which there were several, but had instead become a prominent member of a Christian group which avoided speaking about Christianity and warfare.

I want to know what it takes to make a deeply unpopular decision at a time of national crisis. It seems to me that war creates a narrative of nationalism and patriotism in order to recruit fighters for its cause. Dissenting against that kind of propaganda requires a stubborn bravery all of its own. The closest I've come to this sort of dilemma was during the Falklands War in 1982. There was a period when conscription was being actively talked about and I wondered what I would do. It seemed a poor cause and I was opposed to the serving Conservative government. I remember feeling very awkward, studying at a university in England when the Welsh colony of Patagonia was siding with the Argentine government's claim on the south Atlantic islands.

But my principles and zeal at that time could not be compared to my father's at the same age. I didn't want my life disrupted and the thought of killing another human being filled me then, and still does, with feelings of disgust. But the moment never arose and no decision was ever asked of me.

But it was required of my father and he said no.

CHAPTER 18

1944, a Deep-Rooted Problem

I'm holding a grey woollen overcoat, single-breasted, made by Dunn and Co, one of my father's favourite gents' outfitters. Purchased in the early years of the twenty-first century, it is the latest in a long line of coats worn by my father, particularly when officiating at funerals and gravesides high on a rain-lashed Welsh valley. In earlier years, coats had been given to him by a friend and business owner who was part of the Christian Brethren movement in Newport, John Capper.

I suspect the history of overcoats began with my Uncle Vincent's generosity in Llanelli, dipping into his stock and selling one to my dad at a great discount or, as likely as not, donating it as a gift. My father also related several coat and shoe stories involving his cousin, the Reverend David Samuel Jones, or D. S. as he was affectionately called. Although he and his wife were poorer than the parish rodents, he several times gave away clothes to passing tramps during the great depression. A coat here, a pair of shoes there. I related some of these tales during a Sunday sermon at my first church in Warminster in 1987. I talked about the occasion when a man of the road called at their home in desperate need of clothing; in fact he was barefoot. Only the day before, D. S.'s wife had bought him a pair of shoes, after saving up for them. Most of their own clothes and footwear were worn through. When the tramp knocked on the door, his wife was out at the time and D. S. gave the man his new shoes without hesitation.

This was not the end of this story. About a year later, D. S. was in London, attending some special meetings in London's Albert Hall where a well-known evangelist was speaking. As he made his way towards the entrance he heard his name being called out by a man standing next to a couple of horses. It was the tramp who had come to his door barefooted, who had moved to London and was working as an ostler. A few of the city's taxis were still horse-drawn and that evening he was caring for the animals whilst the owner attended the meeting. Like a shot D. S. took the reins and gave the man his ticket. Later, when the man came back to relieve D. S., the punchline repeated by Dad, who in turn heard it from D. S., was magnificent: "The man had been soundly converted."

That lunchtime, someone knocked on our door at our home in North Row, Warminster. It was a tramp in need of food and clothing. My wife Clare, always more practical in her holiness than I, fed the desperate man and gave him a coat I'd just been given. D. S. Jones's influence was felt very keenly that day.

I still wear the Dunn and Co coat when officiating at cold and wet funerals.

In 1944, John was five years into his training and finding it hard going. Taking into account his preparatory year at Trefeca College, this was his sixth academic year, with one more to go. He had immersed himself into college life but felt himself mentally and emotionally adrift. The confidence that had buoyed him along only a few years ago was dwindling. His parents were being repeatedly insulted by neighbours on account of his pacifism and the war had entered its sixth year. The longer it continued, the greater the pressure on Mam and Dat; a situation which was causing him to question his cause. Mair's long-term absence at Bletchley Park was also taking its toll. Not only did he miss her company, he realized how reliant he was on her positive attitude and emotional stability.

Left alone without Mair, his default setting was generally morose and probably depressed. This is evidenced by some words written in November 1944, once again on the theme of introspection:

Are we becoming too introspective? There certainly seems to be a very real danger of this, and I cannot but feel that too much engrossment with one's own inner state can create terrible havoc in the soul.

My father's war had also become more than a principled objection. In 1944 he was the student minister of a small church in Bedwas, a small mining village about thirteen miles north-east of Cardiff. During term time his duties involved leading Sunday services, although during the long vacations there was an expectation of pastoral care and other duties. On 28 March he received difficult news after a harrowing ordeal:

It was a Monday and I had a terrible toothache. The worst I'd ever experienced. The pain started on Sunday when I was preaching and leading services in Oakdale, high up in the Gwent valleys. I was staying overnight with an elderly couple and by Monday the pain was unbearable. It needed dealing with immediately and they arranged an emergency appointment with the village dentist. I've always had a phobia of dentists and in those days there was no anaesthetic offered to patients. My first impressions of the establishment were not favourable. It was poorly equipped, badly lit and had a squalid air about it.

The dentist was waiting for me; a jovial and portly man, but his manner didn't settle my nerves. I sat in the barber's chair as requested and the dentist got to work. He located the offending tooth, which was towards the back of my lower set, and diagnosed that it needed to come out immediately. I braced myself as he reached for the appliance needed for this procedure. It probably had a particular name but it bore a horrid resemblance to pliers. This wasn't my first extraction and I knew what to expect. I waited for the sensation of cold metal, extreme pressure and the inevitable pain. Nevertheless I was in such anguish at this point that I simply wanted relief. He started on me; pulling, twisting, wrenching, but all to no avail.

"It's too deep rooted," he said to me. "I'm going to get help across the road." He had reached the point of no return. The tooth was half out, blood was filling my mouth and I sat there in what I can only describe as total pain waiting for his return.

He came back with a young man whom he introduced as his son-in-law; the local butcher. "He's got strong arms, we'll have it out in no time," he said cheerily. The son-in-law came into my view and his profession became clear; he was wearing a white apron smeared with fresh blood. His skill in butchering dead sheep and cows would now be applied to my mouth. His movement was swift. He raised his knee to my chest and took hold of the pliers at the same time. With a sudden and forceful jerk, I felt the broken and stubborn root rip out of my mouth. It was agony and ecstasy at the same time.

I have no idea how I left that place of horror or how indeed I managed to catch the next train to Cardiff, but I did. The other passengers must have wondered what kind of creature was sharing their carriage; my head was wrapped in a bandage and my mouth was full of cotton wool. And I was aware of constantly mopping blood from the side of my swollen mouth.

When John arrived back at the college on Richmond Road, the principal greeted him with sobering news:

He'd received a phone call from the church in Bedwas. A young woman who was soon to get married had been working at the Royal Ordinance Factory (ROF) in the city the previous evening. During the night shift a shell exploded in the factory killing one man, his daughter and seven other women. One of these was the young church member known to me. The church did not have its own minister and the family requested that I take the funeral, which had been hastily arranged for the following day.

It emerged that the shell explosion at the ROF was caused by so-called friendly fire. An anti-aircraft gun had been fired from nearby Gabalfa and instead of locating the *Luftwaffe*, this rogue missile found its way a mile away, killing nine people.

On the day of the funeral I was in severe pain as a result of the extraction. I had contracted a fever overnight and knew that something had gone wrong. My mouth was swollen and I felt I could barely speak but I was honour bound to lead this tragic funeral. Somehow God gave me the strength to lead the service but I felt as though I might faint at any time. No one noticed my discomfiture; everyone was filled with sorrow at this tragic death. The church was full and there was a large crowd gathered outside paying their respects. The local MP was present as well as senior staff from the ROF. It felt so pointless and reinforced everything I believed about the wrongness of war. To talk of sides is so misleading when these weapons of death didn't discriminate between innocence and guilt. They killed everyone unfortunate enough to fall across their path. And I must confess to feeling angry during the service. Here in front of me were politicians, military officers and civil servants, who had made certain calculations about the war. In order to gain "victory" they knew that lives would be lost on the British side and they had accepted this young woman's death as part of that price. I really wanted to say something from the pulpit but of course I didn't.

Later that day, John admitted himself to the dental hospital in Cardiff to receive remedial treatment for the incomplete extraction begun two days earlier. A part of the root still needed to be removed and he was given penicillin to deal with the resulting infection.

In November, the same month as his diary entry, John also received a letter from Mair, the first in several months. It was unusually short and its contents alarmed him. The handwriting was spindly, indicating physical weakness. She referred to feelings of exhaustion, from working long hours in a cramped environment. But none of this was new to John. He was however alarmed to learn she feared that her old enemy, influenza, might have returned and she was looking forward to a rest at Christmas.

In December, John received a surprise visit from Mair's father, Dada. He looked ashen-faced and grim as he told John that Mair had been rushed to Aylesbury General Hospital with pneumonia. He had been summoned to the hospital and feared the worst. Dada had been a widower for several years and now dreaded that another life would be taken from him. Both men knew there was no available treatment for viral pneumonia and barring a miracle or good fortune, Mair probably wouldn't pull through.

A week later he was visited again by Dada, who said that Mair's condition was stable but serious. She could yet die, particularly if she fell prey to another infection in hospital. Between Christmas and New Year, John made arrangements to visit Mair in hospital. He was under no illusions that this could be the last time he saw her alive.

None of this is mentioned in his diary for this year or the next.

CHAPTER 19

Not Fit for Human Occupation

Extract from sermon notes, translated by the author from Welsh into English:

Palm Sunday 1965

Luke 19:41

In one of his poems, William Wordsworth says that

"In that sweet mood when pleasant thoughts
Bring sad thoughts to the mind."

The poet in question enjoyed the peace and beauty of the countryside; around him was nature in all its glory. And yet as his soul reacted to this beauty, he found himself thinking about other scenes; over the Channel in France there was warfare and cruelty.

"and much it grieved my heart to think
What man has made of man,"

In these superlative words, Wordsworth expresses feelings
that are universally true. My mind goes back to the end of
the war, when I had accepted the call to Calvary and was
looking forward to starting my ministry there. Germany
had already surrendered, as did Japan within a few weeks.
The church was keen to hold a thanksgiving service to thank
God for his great mercy. I travelled up from Cardiff to lead
the service and later I went back to the church secretary's
house and enjoyed their hospitality. Late into the evening I
looked out of the window and saw that everyone was out in
the streets celebrating the victory. People were coming from
all directions in great joy because they had been released
from all their worst fears and trials. We all felt this great
happiness. But in the midst of this happiness, there was also
a sense of tremendous sadness; sadness at the thought of the
millions that had died and that two Christian countries had
dropped atom bombs on Hiroshima and Nagasaki.

"In that sweet mood when pleasant thoughts
Bring sad thoughts to the mind."

… I'm sure we can all bring to mind strong memories with
their mixed emotions on a day such as this. On Palm Sunday
we rejoice as we remember our dear parents and we treasure
each memory. And yet even in the dearest remembrance
there is a terrible longing [in Welsh, the word hiraeth is a
mixture of longing, homesickness, and grief].

Once again I can hear my father's voice in these words spoken in 1965. By then we had moved to Llanelli where he was leading a Welsh-speaking church. This powerful mix of pathos and memory was a trademark of his oratory.

By 1945, John and Mair's war had turned a corner. Despite the savage pneumonia that attacked her lungs and weakened her already exhausted body, Mair pulled through. Within a few months she returned home, and her war was over. Like that of many other BP staff members, her health had wilted before the bunting of VE Day.

A date was set for their wedding and my father prepared for his final university exams. This was also the year when he had to find a church. Offers of a pastorate had been made to him in the last six years, including one from a church in Hereford, who offered him a post even before he started his formal training. All had been politely declined but this was now the business end of his training; he was getting married and he needed to find a job.

After visiting the church on a few occasions, John received an invitation to the pastorate of Calvary Baptist Church, Trefforest, a small mining village twelve miles north of Cardiff and less than a mile outside Pontypridd. Before accepting the invitation, he was summoned to Principal Chance's study:

*He knew of Calvary and spoke highly of the church but he
also felt that I might be limiting my options. He referred
again to the Baptist college in New Zealand that were seeking
a lecturer with a view to becoming Principal and he felt sure
that my application would be favourably received. He even
suggested that I could pursue a PhD through Cardiff whilst
working in New Zealand. Noting my muted reaction he then
suggested that I simply stay on at the college and pursue a*

PhD at the university in Cardiff. It was very tempting and I greatly enjoyed academic study but I declined his suggestions. Mair and I were getting married and it was important that I could support a family and also I knew I was called to be a church minister. My passion was preaching the gospel and being a shepherd to God's people. I even felt convinced we were meant to stay in Wales.

So it was in January 1945 that the members of the church in Trefforest voted to extend an invitation to John to become the church's next minister. The minutes of that church meeting record:

The recommendation of the Diaconate to invite Mr Russell Jones (student of Cardiff Baptist College) to the pastorate of this church was unanimously carried, having been proposed by Miss Edith Jones and seconded by Miss Nancy Parker. Subject to his agreeing, it was suggested that until the completion of his college course in June, he, Mr Jones, be asked to give two Sundays a month to the church, the stipend to be £3 per Sunday (it was probable he would also come up for some of the week nights). It was agreed to offer a salary of twenty pounds per calendar month as from July. The chairman (Mr ET Jenkins) and the Secretary (WW Evans) were deputed to arrange for an interview with Mr Jones, conveying the invitation to the Pastorate.

On VE Day, 8 May 1945, John attended a street party in Pontycymer with Mair, where they announced the date of their wedding as 26 February 1946. The joy of the occasion was marred by the hostile reaction of Mair's aunts to his presence and the announcement:

Mair had warned me about her powerful aunts but I'd given it very little thought. In fact I thought she was exaggerating, but from the time I arrived I sensed their hostility to me. They were a motley bunch I must say: dressed uniformly in black; widow's weeds you might say. Nothing I said or did could thaw the ice; in fact when they realised I was a conscientious objector they were positively caustic. Mair of course was livid with them, but she later explained that there were many reasons for their antipathy. They had disagreed with her departure for Mount Hermon so soon after her mother died, indicating that her place was at home looking after her father. And then when she returned only to leave again for university they once again voiced their opposition. They also took exception to her faith and the way she spoke openly about her conversion. They were of the opinion that being a Presbyterian and a Christian were the same thing whereas dear Mair reminded them all too frequently that the two things were not synonymous. And to cap it all and make matters worse, she was getting married to a Baptist minister who had refused to fight in the war!

John would be leading a church of about 500 members and his predecessor had recently died in office, having served for over fifty years. The church had a proud tradition of choral singing, dramatic societies, and uniformed organizations. One of the naughtier young boys in the Boys' Brigade had already caught John's attention:

He was lively and full of mischief but in all fairness he'd come from a background of poverty. He was so naughty I had to visit the home a few times and even by the standards of the time, their needs were very great.

The boy in question was Thomas Jones Woodward, later to become the singing sensation Sir Tom Jones.

Several of the church's young men were in the forces, soon to return home. There were plans afoot for a welcome home party, which John of course was expected to lead. And this church had a proud military past – its organ was installed in memory of the fallen of the First World War. There were expectations of a figurehead who would welcome the heroes and speak warmly of their service. This he did without any reference to his own views on warfare.

Along with others, John's reaction to the war's ending was a mixture of relief and joy. In a sermon preached in 1945 he made a reference to something he had noticed above someone's front door:

While travelling the other day, my attention was directed to a certain house. It was an ordinary house in an ordinary street; there was nothing to distinguish it from the other houses – nothing, that is, except for one thing. Above the front door were the remains of a banner which must have been hanging there for some time – the type of thing we used to see when a son or husband used to come back on leave from active service abroad, bearing the inscription in bold letters WELCOME HOME. In this particular instance, however, three of the letters had been obliterated so that the inscription now read COME HOME.

It seemed to me that that banner and its desire were parabolic, and I thought of the houses and homes where such an emblem might be very suitable. We live in days of turmoil and upheaval and one of the institutions that have suffered most from the present unrest is the home. Day by

*day we read in the newspapers and see for ourselves the way
in which homes are being broken up. How many children
would be only too glad to welcome a father back home? How
many wives and husbands would give anything to see their
partners coming back to them? How many mothers' eyes
are red with weeping for a son or daughter who has kicked
over the traces and wandered off to a life of recklessness and
crime?*

Within a few weeks of commencing his post, John conducted his
first wedding ceremony on an unusually warm autumn day:

*Both bride and groom were understandably nervous, and
so was I as I faced my first marriage service. The groom
had recently returned from the forces but the couple had
grown up within a few streets of each other. As soon as the
vows started I knew there would be problems. Whether he
had a slight speech impediment or was simply terrified, the
poor man struggled to say that he would take her to be his
lawfully wedded wife. Despite my most patient efforts, he
kept on repeating that she would be his awfully wedded
wife. Eventually we completed the ceremony and I felt relief
as I got to the prayer of blessing. However as I prayed I felt
pressure on my elbow but thought nothing of it and kept on
praying. But the pressure turned to tugging and I opened my
eyes to see the bride lying prostrate before me. Overwhelmed
by emotion and nerves, she had fainted and I asked the
groom to get his wife a glass of water. On his return from
the kitchen he walked back hurriedly to his groggy wife and
proceeded to throw the water over her!*

As he acquainted himself with pastoral ministry, John came across plenty of situations where war had left its ugly mark on families. His objection to military combat remained but was now sublimated through helping others dealing with its distress. This ability to switch between preacher and pastor was one of his distinctive features. On a whole range of moral issues he could seem fixed and harsh from the pulpit, but in someone's living room listening to their plight, his approach was person-centred and compassionate. For example, he was strictly teetotal, believing it was incumbent on all serious Christians to abstain from the evils of drink. However, over the course of his ministry, he helped numerous families struggling with the issue of alcoholism. And they received from him the gifts of time and grace. He did not scold or even direct them; he simply sat, listened, and prayed.

John moved into the accommodation provided for him. It was a small, damp flat overlooking the River Taff. There was condensation, distemper, and on the ground floor an old widow dying of stomach cancer. This felt a long way from the polished wood of the Baptist college. As men returned from the forces and families were reunited, John settled into his new work.

On 26 February 1946, Mair and John were married in Christchurch, Bridgend, and the officiating minister was his second cousin, the Reverend D. S. Jones.

This is how Dad remembered that day, thirty-seven years later in 1983:

Saturday 26 February 1983

Thirty seven years ago, on this very date, Mair and I were married at Christchurch, Bridgend. Sadly there is no longer a Baptist cause there, but its founder and its only minister was

DS Jones, a cousin of my father's and a brother of the great WS Jones. He was getting on in years when he officiated at our wedding and got into a bit of a muddle with Mair's name especially – I'm rather glad the modern craze for taping services of that nature was not then even dreamt of! – But I'm glad that the old saint was able to be with us.

It doesn't seem possible that 37 years have gone by since that wintry day, and yet five lovely children and three beautiful grandchildren and a rather creaking frame bear their own testimony. Since then not only DS but Nancy and Elsby and Mam and Dat and Elvet Cox have "gone on before". But the God who brought Mair and me together and gave us each other has unfailingly led and supported us, in health and in sickness, and in sorrow, in storm and in sunshine. Our ministry for and with our Lord has been a joint ministry and I can but give humble and sincere thanks for the loyal support of my darling Mair. Her understanding and patience, her wisdom and love have been a constant comfort and inspiration. Without her, my shortcomings would be even more pronounced and my failures even more numerous. Our homes in Trefforest, Aberystwyth, Risca, Llanelli, Cardiff and Caerphilly have lacked many things, but they have been rich in the qualities that make for family and contentment and for that, M – humanly speaking – is mainly responsible. "She is worth far more than rubies." Her husband has full confidence in her and lacks nothing of value. She brings him good not harm all the days of her life… She is clothed with strength and dignity; she can laugh at the days to come. She speaks with wisdom, and faithful instruction is on her tongue. She watches over the affairs of her household and does not eat the bread of idleness. Her

children arise and call her blessed. Her husband also and he
praises her. Many men do noble things, but you surpass them
all. Diolch Iddo [thanks be to God].

The newly-weds moved into the flat in Trefforest and by the end of
the year Mair was expecting their first child. Elizabeth was born in
June 1947 but their living conditions became a cause for concern.
The damp, unhygienic conditions had worsened and were an
immediate risk to their new baby's health.

The winter of 1947 was savage; the worst in living memory.
The snow started falling before Advent and didn't clear
until Easter had passed. Along with the snow came this
bitter, arctic cold; I've never seen anything like it since in
my lifetime. When the snow fell it settled immediately and
then froze while layers of fresh flakes built on huge walls
of ice. There were drifts taller than men everywhere. Gas
and water pipes were frozen; it was truly dreadful. And of
course we were trying to look after our little baby. But the
flat was dangerously inadequate. Combined with the damp
conditions, the lady downstairs was in her last days and
Elizabeth developed this worrying cough. The doctor came
to visit and he told us that if we stayed in the flat, Elizabeth
would not see her first birthday. I remember him saying that
the building was not fit for human occupation and was a
danger to us all. There was damp everywhere. The walls were
streaming with condensation, the lino was moist and both
Elizabeth and Mair were at risk.

Once the snow began to thaw, the three of them made their way
to Vincent and Madge's house in Llanelli. This would be Mair and

Elizabeth's home until new accommodation could be arranged. Dad stayed in Trefforest and visited his family when he could. Church meeting minutes from the period indicate that my father had raised the issue with the church's officers but progress to find an alternative was slow. In the meantime, after a preaching engagement in Alfred Place Baptist Church, Aberystwyth, he received an invitation to the pastorate, which he accepted.

As he left Trefforest he received a specific greeting from a small group within the church. The young men who had returned from military service wished to thank him for the pastoral care and support which they and their families had received from him.

Chapter 20

A Strange Courage

… Kagawa preached, wrote, and worked unceasingly for the cause of Christian socialism; in 1925 trade unions were given legal right to organise, and in 1926 legislation was finally passed for abolishing the slums. Kagawa made his mark as a mystic, ascetic and pacifist, but it was as a soldier of movements that his influence was greatest. He once stated as his aim the "salvation of 100,000 poor, the emancipation of 9,430,000 labourers and the liberation of twenty million tenant farmers". Prominent as a church leader and patriot, he continued as Japan's apostle of love to the end…[1]

The New International Dictionary of the Christian Church made its first appearance in my father's Cardiff study sometime in 1974. I've chosen this book and period for two reasons. As already mentioned, Dad had a huge regard for Toyohiko Kagawa and his name cropped up time after time during my adolescence. More pressingly, this was an awful period for my parents and one event in particular illustrates my dad's painfully fragile mind. And in my mind, there's a connection between this and his pacifist convictions. Many of the views he held made him feel like an outsider. After a few years in a city centre church, the strain of trying to keep a fragmenting faith community together took its toll. Early in 1975 he suffered periods of depression, acute asthma and angina, and then suffered a full-blown heart attack. He later described his emotional state at that time:

I had to visit a local psychiatric hospital as one of our members was a patient there at the time. After one such visit, I went back to the car but found myself pacing up and down the pavement instead of driving away. I looked longingly at the red brick Victorian hospital with its green dome and thought to myself, "That's where I should be." I felt so lonely, so useless in many ways. My work as a minister was beginning to crush me and there seemed to be so many people against me. I had this dreadful feeling that the people inside that hospital were better off than me and that if I could only admit myself I would be better off.

After his heart attack, he returned home for a brief period before being rushed back into hospital. This time it was worse. He had something called a pulmonary embolism; a clot on the lung in layman's terms. That summer dragged, as it was expected that he would not survive. One cough, sudden movement, or random event could snuff him out. My mother told us to expect the worst but this didn't stop the church he was leading passing a vote of no confidence in him. Caught between life and death, work and unemployment, Dad was fighting for his life with the church around his neck. Eventually his condition improved and he came home, frailer and thinner than I remembered him. And he seemed vulnerable and needy. One evening we were alone together in the lounge watching TV, sitting on the sofa. Inexplicably he came closer and rested his head on my shoulder. We said nothing; I think he just needed some warmth and security from a fellow creature.

The summer of 1974 has been in my thoughts most of the time I've been writing this book. And to my mind at least there's an association between Dad's broken heart and the unbearable inner tension he'd bottled up inside. Throughout his life, he was a man of strong opinions and some of them brought him into conflict with others; but mostly with himself. He internalized his tension, felt the rejection of his peers, squashed it down, and tried to carry on as normal. As his reputation grew, particularly in Wales, he became a well-known champion of conservative evangelical theology, although he retained an admiration for people whose views were the polar opposite of his tribe. And he ended up abandoning these tribes, some of which he'd helped establish. He was a defender of traditional sexual morality but nevertheless understood the dilemmas faced by young people, and he conceded that there were occasions when abortion was acceptable.

Most profoundly he had been a pacifist at a time when many Christians around him argued in favour of a just war and thus endorsed Christian military service. His anti-war stance was fired in the furnace of radical politics and a theology which embraced the fatherhood of God and the brotherhood of man. He saw himself part of a movement intent on bringing the kingdom of God to earth, uniting a divided church around a common cause. And then he fell in love with Calvinism, with its systematic theology and gloomy vision of a depraved humanity. He became a lonely pacifist marooned on his own intellectual sandbank;

and he journeyed inwards and downwards seeking a closer walk with God. I think my father was ill at ease with his large imagination and felt guilty for thinking too widely and feeling too deeply. Sensitive to the opinions of others, holding on to his own convictions, the only way he could deal with his own warring soul was through keeping a largely silent and diplomatic front.

My parents were married for sixty-four years before Dad's death on 28 February, St David's Day eve, in 2011. Mair passed away on 28 December 2013, living to hear the good news of the safe delivery of her new twin great-granddaughters but not long enough to see the publication of the book she inspired. During their six and a half decades together as man and wife they produced five children (Elizabeth, Helen, David, Iwan, and Gethin) and became grandparents to a further fifteen (Gethin, Rachel, Judith, Alistair, Gareth, Anna, Bronwen, Thomas, Adam, Gruffydd, Meredydd, Martha, Dafydd, Sian, and Bryn). And when their first great-grandson, Dylan, was born, they shared the universal joy of great-grandparents everywhere. My mother alone rejoiced in Katie and Isla's arrival forming now a trinity of great-grandchildren.

This book has been a personal quest, an attempt to piece the fragments together and make more of a jigsaw and less of a puzzle. I've tried to find the man inside the Conchie; the old, old story of a son trying to understand his dad. I've uncovered plenty of stories that were new to me. Everyone's life is essentially a mystery, its meaning elusive sometimes even to them, but I feel I've lifted the lid on my dad's strange courage.

What has been the legacy of his pacifism within our family? My dad was only twenty-one when he came out and declared his radical views; men of his age and younger were fighter pilots, sailors, soldiers, and spies. It was a young war. So what impact has my father's war had on the rest of us? Since World War Two, Britain has been at war on numerous occasions, sometimes against itself. The troubles in Northern Ireland, Falklands War, wars in the Gulf, Iraq, Afghanistan, and Kosovo have afforded plenty of opportunity for military service as professionals or territorials but none has been taken. This may not be unusual but none of my siblings and their offspring have shown the slightest interest in the armed forces. And the issue of legacy is not at all straightforward, bound up as it is within a framework of faith. Whereas about half the family would describe themselves as Christians, the others would probably define their religious convictions in other ways.

A number of the anecdotes and fragments of memory found in these pages come from my sisters and brothers. For example, the story about Mam being given a white feather as a symbol of my dad's cowardice comes from my younger sister, Helen. Our oldest sister, Elizabeth, has filled in many of the gaps surrounding John's early home life in Gorseinon.

I've noticed that some within the immediate and wider family were barely aware of his pacifism. Some who were small children at the time when war broke out recalled that Uncle John had made this stance but had no particular memories of its impact on their lives, or those of their parents. Neither I nor anyone else I've asked can remember him defending or stating his pacifist beliefs beyond the home environment. This is understandable; so it is with most of the values we hold dear to us, except my father had a weekly public platform from which he spoke more or less every Sunday and a few times every midweek for at least fifty years. He gave thousands of addresses, spanning five decades, to small and large congregations alike, and there isn't a single record of a public pronouncement.

My younger brother Iwan however comments on some of our dad's sermon notes on 1 Peter which he came across:

> I think these were preached in 1947 or 1948 since they mention contemporary meetings in London related to the formation of the United Nations. There's strong critique of the "brotherhood of man, fatherhood of God" doctrine – certainly no sign of liberalism here. But then he goes on in the next sermon to address human selfishness and the radicalism of the Gospel by contrast – and the sacrificial love of Christ that is demanded of his people.

Iwan has read other sermons from that period and makes the following comments:

> So I don't think he abandons his pacifism at any point. He just never sees it as a programme, a viable political strategy. Dad refused to regard any ism – including pacifism – as capable of solving the human problem. I think that in this he was probably influenced at an early stage of his studies in Cardiff not only by the outlook of Reformed evangelicals like Martyn Lloyd Jones but also by the writings of continental thinkers like Karl Barth and Emil Brunner, both of whose books were well represented on his shelves and whom he certainly would have encountered early on through his teachers in Cardiff, especially someone like Theodore Robinson who had studied in Germany.
>
> Barth drew attention to the crisis of Western civilization, the failure of liberal ideas of progress and human advancement, and the arrogance and pride at the heart of the cultural enterprise. Dad was fond of the quote about

World War I as "the war to end all wars" – and he used this regularly to draw attention to wishful thinking, and to reject any kind of humanistic solutions which fail to confront the reality of sin in human life. I think that a powerful influence upon him here was Barth's critique of nineteenth-century German liberal theology which, in fact, emerged very clearly out of World War I, when many of the great liberal theologians like his teacher, Adolf von Harnack, lined up to support the Kaiser and the German war.

Reflecting on Dad's pacifist influence on himself and his offspring, my older brother David (who now lives in New Zealand) says:

I remember seeing some of his books – though I didn't read them – either by or about Bonhoeffer – and knew that this was a pacifist who plotted against Hitler. I'm pretty sure that I missed out in not taking advantage of his library as he was such a disciplined thinker who deeply understood logic and ethics.

I remember buying *Commando* war comics and bringing them home to read. Dad never indicated that he disliked them, or even that he noticed their presence in the house, and his main plan of attack must have been his incessant encouragement to read classical literature instead. I did that as well, but liked the variety of those little A5-size picture magazines.

Despite this lack of overt messaging from him, there were some pointers such as his lack of enthusiasm towards uniformed organizations in his churches, with no encouragement heading our way to get involved in such activities.

I don't recall him showing disrespect towards the British Legion or veterans from WW2, but again I have no memories about being encouraged to attend Remembrance Day services. Here in New Zealand, ANZAC Day dawn services are attended by thousands and I have attended a few, something I would never have considered in the UK, partly because of my probably bigoted perception of the Legion as being a bunch of reactionary old Tories.

On the other hand I was aware of his leftist inclinations and during my teenage years began to assume that his views about war were also impacted by the use of the military in domestic affairs – the Tonypandy Riots, for example. The dignity of labour meant more to him than the savagery of war, and to be a hero was to look after your butties down the pit as much as on the battlefield.

I don't ever remember a discussion about the death penalty but I know without doubt that he was heavily against it and would never support that ultimate sanction, however serious the offence.

Whatever Dad said, or didn't say, I ended up becoming a pacifist myself, and am convinced that I reached that path directly because of him. The Ten Commandments – along with the injunctions of other world religions – emphasise personal responsibility in many areas of human activity and Dad passed on to all his children that key message.

Today, I am delighted that all four of my children have developed similar views of their own. None of them share Dad's Christian perspective (and neither do I) but they all care deeply about poverty, citizenship, and the rights of minorities. All of these are areas where Dad had strong, unshakeable values which left a strong mark on me, as well as being conveyed through his personality to his grandchildren.

At the end of this quest, am I any clearer about my father's motives as a Conchie? Recognizing the impossibility of distilling a life to a few thousand words, I believe that my dad's objection to war was essentially a very personal expression of faith. Unlike other COs he did not identify with specific anti-war campaigns or join a political party. Like Groucho Marx he would probably have felt uneasy in any club or movement that would have him as a member. Of this I am clear: my father was no coward. Walking against the tide of militarism took a different kind of courage and for him it was an integral part of his Christian discipleship. The way of Christ was the way of the cross and this was the one he had to carry.

I have attempted to write this account in the spirit of one of my father's favourite quotations, attributed to Oliver Cromwell on having his portrait painted:

> Mr Lely, I desire you would use all your skill to paint your picture truly like me, and not flatter me at all; but remark all these roughness, pimples, warts and everything as you see me; otherwise I will never pay a farthing for it.

In a final ironic twist, as this book was being written, the world was reminded of the seventy-fifth anniversary of the catastrophic act that ended the Second World War. On 6 August 1945 an atom bomb fell on the Japanese city of Hiroshima, killing an estimated 140,000 people out of a population of 350,000. Three days later and another American bomb was dropped on Nagasaki, killing a further 70,000. In 2015 bells were rung and the nation remembered in silence. We were witnessing the grief of the world's only country where pacifism is written into their constitution. Strange that the Christianity that cradled my dad continues to stockpile weapons of mass destruction, whereas Shinto has turned the other cheek.

Notes

Chapter 2: Conchie
1. Morris, Gareth, *A Llanelli Boy*, p. 94.

Chapter 4: Strong Mothers
1. Stowe, Harriet Beecher, *Uncle Tom's Cabin*, London: Dean and Son, 1934.

Chapter 5: Hovel Fit for a King
1. Davies, D. Tom, "The Industrial Revolution in Tir Y Brenin (Gorseinon)", http://gorseinontowncouncil.bayviewcms.com/gorseinon-district-history/page3_gorseinon.php (Accessed 11 December 2015).

Chapter 6: I Was in School with Him
1. http://www.swansearfc.co.uk/Page/Content/827 (Accessed 11 December 2015).

2. Gilbert, Martin, *Prophet of Truth. Winston S. Churchill, vol. 5, 1922–1939*, London: Minerva, 1990, p. 456.

3. http://www.ppu.org.uk/learn/infodocs/people/pst_dick.html (Accessed 14 December 2015).

Chapter 7: John the Baptist
1. Clark, Glenn, *Silver Sandals*, http://www.cfointernational.org/wp-content/uploads/2011/03/Silver-Sandals.pdf, p. 8.

2. Kagawa, Toyohiko, quoted in Foreword to *Silver Sandals*, http://www.cfointernational.org/wp-content/uploads/2011/03/Silver-Sandals.pdf (Accessed 11 December 2015).

3. Lester, Muriel, quoted at Fellowship of Reconciliation, http://forusa.org/blogs/for/peace-quotes-muriel-lester/10227 (Accessed 11 December 2015).

Chapter 8: 1936 and the Rise of Nationalism

1. Evans, Gwynfor, *Heddychiaeth Gristnogol yng Nghymru* (Christian Pacifism in Wales), Cymdeithas y Cymod, p. 20.

Chapter 9: 1938, a Year of Preparation

1. http://www.sacred-texts.com/chr/barmen.htm (Accessed 14 December 2015), quoting from Cochrane, Arthur C., *The Church's Confession Under Hitler*, Philadelphia: PA: Westminster Press, 1962, pp. 237–42.

2. http://www.sacred-texts.com/chr/barmen.htm.

Chapter 11: 1939, Cardiff 9050

1. Morrison, Charles Clayton, *The Christian Century*, 7 July 1910.

Chapter 12: 1940, Air Raid Warden

1. Lloyd Jones, Martyn, *Why Does God Allow War?: A General Justification of the Ways of God*, London: Hodder and Stoughton, 1939.

2. Lloyd Jones, Martyn, "He is Our Peace", in *The Christ-Centered Preaching of Martyn Lloyd Jones: Classic Sermons for the Church Today*, Elizabeth Catherwood and Christopher Catherwood (eds), Wheaton, IL: Crossway, 2014, p. 188.

Chapter 14: Let Me Now Be God's Soldier

1. Macgregor, G. H. C., *The New Testament Basis of Pacifism*, 1936, p. 147.

2. Justin Martyr, in *The Ante-Nicene Fathers*, vol. 1, Edinburgh: T&T Clark, 1867, p. 254.

3. Origen, *Contra Celsus*, Book 8, chap. 73, translated in *The Ante-Nicene Fathers*, vol. 4, Edinburgh: T&T Clark, 1873. See: http://www.earlychristianwritings.com/text/celsus2.html (Accessed 14 December 2015).

4. Sulpicius Severus, *Life of St. Martin*, 4.

5. Hershberger, Guy Franklin, *War, Peace, and Nonresistance*, Scottsdale, PA: The Herald Press, 1944, pp. 22–23.

6. Bowman, Rufus D., *The Church of the Brethren and War, 1708–1941*, Elgin, IL: Brethren Publishing House, 1944, p. 268.

7. "A Declaration from the Harmless and Innocent People of God, Called Quakers, London: 1660", quoted in *Margaret Fell's Letter to the King on Persecution, 1660*, ed. Britain Yearly Meeting.

8. http://www.for.org.uk/who/history/ (Accessed 17 December 2015).

Chapter 15: 1943, a Badly Chewed Suit
1. Cave, Sydney, *Christianity and Some Living Religions of the East*, London: Duckworth, 1929, p. 212.

Chapter 16: 1944, a Love Letter to Piety
1. Dudley-Smith, Timothy, *John Stott: The Making of a Leader*, Leicester: IVP, 1999.

2. Himbury, D. M., *History of South Wales Baptist College*, Abertawe: Ty Ilston, 1950.

Chapter 20: A Strange Courage
1. Part of Toyohiko Kagawa's citation in *The New International Dictionary of the Christian Church*, Exeter: Paternoster Press, 1974.

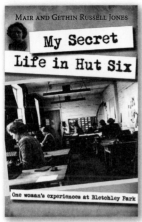

Born and brought up in the sheltered environment of the Welsh valleys, Mair Thomas is amazed to discover her grasp of the German language and musical training make her an ideal code-breaker for Bletchley Park. Leaving behind disapproving aunts and her pacifist boyfriend, she finds herself working long shifts in Hut Six. Sworn to secrecy, she is so afraid of blurting out something she shouldn't that she cannot sleep, especially not when her landlord threatens to lurk outside her door to check whether she talks in her sleep.

Despite cramped and uncomfortable working conditions, Mair came to value her days at Bletchley more than any others in her life. She vividly captures an era of danger and day-to-day challenges, with the constant strain occasionally brightened by visits from the top brass, including Churchill. This first-hand account, remembered affectionately by Mair, and painstakingly recorded by her son, Gethin, gives a fascinating insight into one woman's war.

> **"An absorbing read which gets closer to the humdrum reality of war."**
>
> *Derek Wilson, historian and author*

> **"An engaging account of life at the heart of one of Britain's most important operations during the Second World War. I greatly enjoyed this book."**
>
> *Edward Stourton, broadcaster and author*

ISBN: 978-0-7459-5664-0
e-ISBN: 978-0-7459-5665-7